The Unnecessary War

misperception?

Contents

Assessors:
Dr Malcolm Dando, School of Peace Studies, Bradford University
(Chairman)
Professor John Ferguson, President, The Selly Oak Colleges,
1979-86
Richard Baker, Ex-Assistant Secretary Civil Service, and former
Head of Department, Sheffield Polytechnic

Preface

These Proceedings, of the 2-day Belgrano Enquiry held in November 1986 at Hampstead Town Hall, will we hope further an understanding as to why Britain went to war over the Falkland Islands. It was the collective view of the Belgrano Action Group, who organised the event, that crucial facts about the origins of the war and the steps which might have been taken to prevent it had been deliberately concealed. Many crucial facts remain concealed to this day, and official secrets continue to obfuscate key issues, yet it was our view that enough of the story had emerged to make possible a public Enquiry.

Distinguished experts, many of whom have written books on the subject, have here expressed their candid opinions, and have by no means always agreed with each other. Was the Belgrano sunk because, as Tam Dalyell has argued, Mrs Thatcher wished to block a peace plan and have a war, for political reasons — or, was it rather that the navy was pre-empting political decisions because it needed some action to stave off cuts? These transcripts are of especial interest because many of the experts have here been prepared to express themselves in a more forthright manner than in writing hitherto. Government experts declined to attend, but we attempted as far as possible to obtain a balanced assessment.

Some fresh information was presented, of particular interest being evidence concerning the dimensions of the nuclear threat which accompanied the Task Force into the South Atlantic. Several witnesses described how a strategic nuclear threat was deployed against a non-nuclear power in the Falklands War. This indicated that Britain breached the Treaty of Tlatelolco, which prohibits any nuclear weapons around the continent of South America.

'Disinformation' was the word which one of our witnesses used to describe the evidence which senior persons gave to the Foreign Affairs Committee Report of 1985, concerning the events surrounding the sinking of the Belgrano. Much vital information did however emerge from that Report, and it has been a basis for structuring the present Enquiry. Its Minority Report by Opposition members raised centrally important questions concerning the manner in which the war was precipitated, and these have never been debated in the Commons.

Britain continues to pay £250 million a year to sustain a 'fortress Falklands' situation, in which the relevant UN resolutions continue not to be implemented, and which is entirely unfeasible in the long-term. *There is no stable peace*: five years after the conflict broke out, Costa Mendez the former Foreign Minister of Argentina said that in the South Atlantic: 'confrontation is today as serious, or more serious than before April 2nd.'

The Falklands' Conflict, it can be argued, transformed the most unpopular British Prime Minister since opinion polls began into one surrounded by a mantle of triumph and glory who could then remain in office for longer than anyone else this century. It is the duty of citizens to be concerned about the extent to which they were deceived in this process. This has been a citizens' Enquiry, organised by persons with no party-political axe to grind, made possible entirely by voluntary donations and conducted over Remembrance Week of the International Year of Peace. We would like to thank all the people who made the Enquiry possible, especially Camden Borough Council for their grant of £500, the Mayor of Camden for opening the event, and the witnesses and Assessors for giving so freely of their time, and Tim Langford of Multiple Image Productions Ltd for filming the events.

A short video is available for hire from Concord Films Council Ltd.

Diana Gould,
Ted Haywood,
Nick Kollerstrom,
Duncan Smith,   **Belgrano Action Group Committee**

Introduction

For five years the 'Belgrano' has been the issue in British politics that will not go away despite all the efforts of the Government to kill it.

At the start the Government was defensive about what had been done and a series of lies led to a two year long systematic cover-up designed to stop Parliament and people from finding out the truth. When I revealed the truth to an MP I was immediately prosecuted in a trial which the Government ensured was held partly in camera. The Foreign Affairs Select Committee investigated but the government supporters on the committee ensured that key witnesses were not called and difficult questions not asked. That report and the minority report have never been debated in Parliament.

Key documents have gone missing or not been revealed. The log book of HMS Conqueror, the submarine that sank the 'Belgrano', had been lost in circumstances that have never been explained and even a months long enquiry by Scotland Yard has found no clues. The crucial diplomatic telegrams over the weekend of the sinking have been concealed. Even when I wrote the Top Secret intelligence report now known as the 'Crown Jewels' I was not allowed to see these telegrams. Similarly the Foreign Affairs Committee was refused access.

No wonder that Michael Heseltine thought that there might be a 'Watergate' in here somewhere. The Belgrano Enquiry is important because all those who were prepared to talk gave evidence and despite every opportunity to do so the Government refused to take part. These papers are therefore the best available summary of what we know at the moment. The full truth may have to wait a little longer.

But the very fact that this enquiry had to take place is a damning indictment of the British political system. If these events had taken place in the United States a full scale Congressional enquiry would have been held with evidence given on oath and the truth might have been found.

In Britain the political system has failed because there is no mechanism for holding an enquiry which the government does not

control. The Government and its supporters want the issue to go
away and most of the opposition see no political advantage in
continually raising the subject. Meanwhile the truth still lies
buried. Let us hope that it does not take thirty years or more for
it to emerge when the careers of those involved no longer matter.
It is time we had a method of holding the Government to account.

Clive Ponting

SEQUENCE OF EVENTS 1-2 MAY 1982

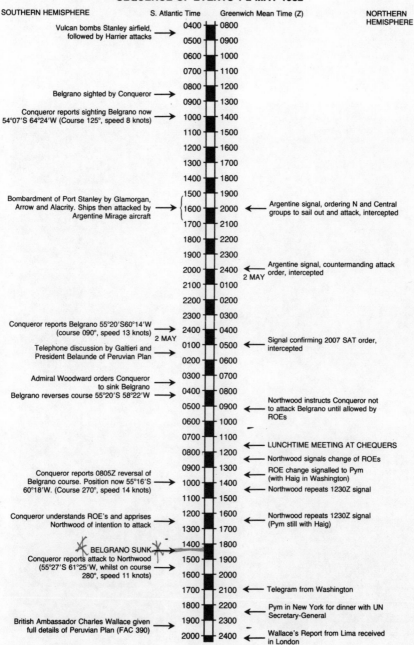

SOUTHERN HEMISPHERE

S. Atlantic Time — Greenwich Mean Time (Z)

NORTHERN HEMISPHERE

S. Atlantic Time	GMT (Z)
0400	0800
0500	0900
0600	1000
0700	1100
0800	1200
0900	1300
1000	1400
1100	1500
1200	1600
1300	1700
1400	1800
1500	1900
1600	2000
1700	2100
1800	2200
1900	2300
2000	2400 (2 MAY)
2100	0100
2200	0200
2300	0300
2400 (2 MAY)	0400
0100	0500
0200	0600
0300	0700
0400	0800
0500	0900
0600	1000
0700	1100
0800	1200
0900	1300
1000	1400
1100	1500
1200	1600
1300	1700
1400	1800
1500	1900
1600	2000
1700	2100
1800	2200
1900	2300
2000	2400

Southern Hemisphere events:

- Vulcan bombs Stanley airfield, followed by Harrier attacks (0400)
- Belgrano sighted by Conqueror (0800)
- Conqueror reports sighting Belgrano now 54°07′S 64°24′W (Course 125°, speed 8 knots) (1000)
- Bombardment of Port Stanley by Glamorgan, Arrow and Alacrity. Ships then attacked by Argentine Mirage aircraft (1600)
- Conqueror reports Belgrano 55°20′S60°14′W (course 090°, speed 13 knots) 2 MAY (2400)
- Telephone discussion by Galtieri and President Belaunde of Peruvian Plan (0100)
- Admiral Woodward orders Conqueror to sink Belgrano (0300)
- Belgrano reverses course 55°20′S 58°22′W (0400)
- Conqueror reports 0805Z reversal of Belgrano course. Position now 55°16′S 60°18′W. (Course 270°, speed 14 knots) (1000)
- Conqueror understands ROE's and apprises Northwood of intention to attack (1200)
- ✠ BELGRANO SUNK. Conqueror reports attack to Northwood (55°27′S 61°25′W, whilst on course 280°, speed 11 knots) (1500)
- British Ambassador Charles Wallace given full details of Peruvian Plan (FAC 390) (1900)

Northern Hemisphere events:

- Argentine signal, ordering N and Central groups to sail out and attack, intercepted (2000)
- Argentine signal, countermanding attack order, intercepted (2400 2 MAY)
- Signal confirming 2007 SAT order, intercepted (0500)
- Northwood instructs Conqueror not to attack Belgrano until allowed by ROEs (0900)
- LUNCHTIME MEETING AT CHEQUERS (1100)
- Northwood signals change of ROEs (1200)
- ROE change signalled to Pym (with Haig in Washington) (1300)
- Northwood repeats 1230Z signal (1400)
- Northwood repeats 1230Z signal (Pym still with Haig) (1600)
- Telegram from Washington (2100)
- Pym in New York for dinner with UN Secretary-General (2200)
- Wallace's Report from Lima received in London (2400)

I

The Background

Malcolm Harper, Michael Harbottle

Malcolm Harper

I'm Malcolm Harper, the Director of the United Nations Association. I want to make one or two very brief background comments to the history of Anglo-Argentine relations between 1833 and 2nd April 1982, because it is quite clear from all the evidence that the basic issue between the two countries for 150 years was ownership of the Falkland Islands and any other problems that arose, arose because of the lack of clarity as to who could justifiably claim sovereignty to the Islands. And I think it's very important in looking at the relationship between the United Kingdom and the United Nations after 2nd April 1982 to be very clear that for many years prior to the invasion, British doubts about British claims to sovereignty of the Islands had been growing rather than decreasing. There is an interesting quote in the Desmond Rice, Arthur Gavshon book, of the Duke of Wellington in the early nineteenth century doubting whether Britain had a really valid claim and that was of course before the 1833 reoccupation. But certainly in 1910 and in 1940 the British had within the Foreign Office really doubted whether they were able to sustain a valid claim of sovereignty. And in the 1970s when David Owen was Foreign Secretary, it was agreed that there should be a fresh round of negotiations with Argentina which included, formally, not only the Falkland Islands but the dependencies as well which came into the reckoning in terms of sovereignty. Since 2nd April 1982 the British Government has apparently been in no doubt whatsoever that British claims to sovereignty are absolute and cannot be challenged. So confident are they that in so far as I am aware, the papers relating to that issue, which were open to public scrutiny in the Public Record Office, were removed from public accessibility, and please correct me if I'm wrong, but when last I made enquiries they were not yet available for the public to look at. And I just have to ask myself the question, if you really believe that your claim is so strong that there is no reason to doubt it, the one thing you want to do is to allow as many people as possible to see the evidence in support of your argument.

Britain in the very early period of April 1982, acted I believe totally in conformity with its responsibilities as a member state of the United Nations. On 1st April Sir Anthony Parsons, the British Ambassador at the United Nations, spoke in the Security Council and warned the Council of what Britain believed was the imminent danger of an Argentine invasion of the Islands and urged that the member states of the United Nations should seek to put pressure on Argentina to desist from any such action. The following day the invasion was accomplished and the United Kingdom went straight back to the Security Council with Resolution 502 drafted in its pocket. And Resolution 502 appeared to be in some doubt of acceptance. As you probably know already there are fifteen members of the UN Security Council and to get a resolution adopted there have to be nine affirmative votes and no veto by any of the five permanent members of the Council. In fact the Resolution was adopted; there was a lot of diplomatic to-ing and fro-ing and the evidence suggests that Uganda and Jordan became key factors in the issue and when their votes were secured in favour of the Resolution it looked as though, subject to no veto presumably by the Soviet Union or possibly China, the Resolution would be adopted. There was no veto and Resolution 502 was adopted.

Resolution 502 made three mandatory demands upon the member states of the United Nations. It demanded an immediate cessation of all hostilities by both sides. It demanded the withdrawal of the Argentine armed forces, and presumably also the civilians who accompanied them, from the Islands. And it demanded the early resumption of renewed dialogue between the two States in order to seek a diplomatic resolution of the crisis. At that point in time I have it on very high evidence from within the Foreign Office, told me off the record and therefore I cannot quote my source, that Britain made the witting decision not to seek to use the machinery of the United Nations any further in trying to find a non-military solution to the conflict in the South Atlantic. The United Kingdom, by that stage had decided to rely heavily on the shuttle diplomacy of Mr Alexander Haig and in comment and question afterwards I think we ought to try to look at the motivation of the United States of America in offering that shuttle diplomacy. This made it extremely difficult for the Secretary General of the United Nations to play an active open role in trying to seek a diplomatic solution to the problems of the South Atlantic in accordance with Resolution 502.

From that moment onwards the United Kingdom also claimed it had acted in sending a Task Force to the South Atlantic strictly within Article 51 of the U.N. Charter which talks of course of the right to self defence in the wake of an attack being launched against your *sovereign* territory. And I stress the word against your sovereign territory because from 2nd April onwards when the papers had been withdrawn from the Public Record Office, the United Kingdom had to argue its unimpeachable sovereignty over the Islands in order to be able to justify its use of force within the terms of Article 51 of the U.N. Charter. And the whole argument which has raged since on the British being justified or not justified in quoting Article 51 has to depend on your opinion as to whether British sovereignty over the Islands was valid or was invalid. If it was invalid then there was no justification for using force within Article 51 because it was not British sovereign territory which had been attacked but was some other sort of territory depending on what your views are.

Such was the isolation, at least at the Whitehall end, of the United Nations, that when towards the end of April the British Foreign Secretary Francis Pym went to the United States of America, again I have it from the same Foreign Office source off the record, he did not actually include the Secretary-General of the United Nations on the list of people with whom he wished to have a discussion while he was in the United States of America. And I understand that it was Sir Anthony Parsons himself who took the initiative of inviting his boss from Whitehall to dinner in his apartment in New York on the Sunday night, which in fact was the night on which the Belgrano had been sunk and the Peruvian Peace Initiative finally seemed to founder. And having invited his boss and being told that Francis Pym would be delighted to come, he then invited the Secretary-General of the United Nations to dinner in his apartment in New York on exactly the same day at exactly the same time in order to make sure that the two men would meet. And if the United Kingdom had been wishing to use the good offices and the initiatives of the U.N. to help to find that diplomatic solution in terms of Resolution 502, then it was a very odd way to go about it that you forgot or whatever, to put the U.N. Secretary-General on your list of people to speak to.

I have to say that it is my personal view, and I think that of many people in U.N.A., that Sir Anthony Parsons, the British Ambassador, was trying, although unofficially, to find ways of mobilising U.N. support for some form of non-military solution to the crisis which the Argentine invasion had created.

What in our view could have happened in the wake of Resolution 502 being adopted was a broad scenario which, in the last two or three minutes I have available, I will briefly try to describe. The United Kingdom with 502 firmly secured in its pocket could have requested a further urgent meeting of the U.N. Security Council

in order to try to put some flesh on the skeleton which 502 had
provided. It could for example have gone back with a draft
resolution which said we are willing not to despatch a military force
at least at this stage to the South Atlantic, but we do require from
the authorities in Buenos Aires a very clear-cut signal that they
are willing to fulfil Article 2 of that Resolution, which was their
withdrawal from the Falkland Islands. And it is not beyond the
wit of humanity, particularly of professional diplomats to be able
to suggest a reasonable timetable during which Argentina should
have shown its willingness to observe that requirement. I cannot
believe that Sir Anthony Parsons could not have proposed that if
within ten or fourteen days there had been no movement of
military personnel and supplies off the Islands, then the British
Government would take it that the Argentine authorities were not
willing to implement Resolution 502. I believe also he could have
said to the American Permanent Representative to the United
Nations, Mrs Jean Kirkpatrick, in a sort of off-the-cuff aside which
was picked up within the Security Council, "If they have any
logistic difficulties in terms of aircraft or ships I'm quite sure that
my good friends in the United States of America would be only
too willing to place at their disposal whatever technology was
required to assist them in that process." It would have been
extremely hard for the Americans to have declined any such
suggestion and I would venture to suggest that it would have placed
on the United States of America a much more urgent requirement
to get a diplomatic solution than Mr Haig was able to secure
through his shuttle diplomacy.

The United Kingdom could also have said at the same time in
that debate that in the event of the Argentine authorities being
unwilling to return to a diplomatic methodology for resolving the
conflict, they would come back without any hesitation to the
Security Council to seek an urgent series of diplomatic, economic,
cultural and other measures in the form of sanctions against the
Argentine Government until such time as it showed itself willing
to conform to the requirements of Resolution 502. And I do
believe that within the U.N. as a whole there would have been
very considerable support for getting Argentina off the hook which
it had put itself on by its invasion by threatening a series of
activities which would have been painful to an already rocky
Argentine Junta, rocky both politically and economically, and
which would have exposed in the international forum of the United
Nations and beyond, the isolation which with the exception of a
series of Latin American countries, I suspect Argentina would
have suffered had that been followed through. If the British
Government still wished at that point to persist with the argument

that sovereignty was unimpeachable it could have said, as an ultimate resort, it would then have to deploy military force in order to evict these unwelcome and illegal occupants of the islands from the Falklands by sending a military Task Force to the region.

I have been given by official sources two reasons why it was not possible to go through with such a scenario. The first is that had such a resolution been put to the Security Council, the Soviet Union which had been caught napping at the time of 502 would undoubtedly have used its veto. When I put that problem to the Soviet U.N.A. in Moscow towards the end of 1982, they doubted very much whether the Soviet Union would have used its veto on this particular issue. When you ask the British Government for the grounds on which it made that assumption, it does not appear that it was because they had hurried negotiations within the U.N. structure with the Soviet Ambassador; it was a guess, that inevitably the Soviet Union would try to make mischief and one way they could do so would be to try to spoil this diplomatic round by using the veto. Their argument they felt was strengthened when they pointed out that at that time the Soviet Union, which had another grain deficit, was in fact negotiating very heavily with Argentina to try and buy surplus grain from Argentina for internal consumption within the Soviet Union, so that they would not wish to upset the Argentines.

That was the first reason given. The second reason given was the season of the year; that we had to get on with the war and get it over because the winter was setting in and if we didn't get it over before the winter set in, it would mean we'd have to wait for several months and then there would be a more full-blown conflict. Our argument is certainly that it was worth at least seriously considering the risk, and many of us would want a fuller commitment than that, to try to avoid armed conflict until the eleventh and a half hour. Even if a final armed conflict had been more bloody than the one which took place, in any case it would have been because every real effort at non-violent conflict resolution had been unsuccessfully exhausted rather than that we were building up a task force right from the word go. And indeed if Gavshon and Rice are to be believed we were building up the task force before the invasion had actually taken place.

My final point is that, by refusing to use the machinery of the United Nations, the British Government, a founder-member and a permanent member of the Security Council, placed the Secretary-General in an almost impossible situation because he was having to try behind the scenes to argue with the Junta in Buenos Aires and with the administration here in London, that they should be using international machinery in order to find a non-violent resolution to the conflict. And it is indeed the Secretary-General of the United Nations or a specially appointed respresentative of his who should have been undertaking the shuttle diplomacy between Buenos Aires and London and not the Secretary of State of the United States administration. But when as powerful a nation as the United States intervenes and takes upon itself that role, it does in terms of real-politik become extremely difficult for the United Nations Secretary-General to run a parallel shuttle diplomacy in competition, which is what it would be, with that of the United States of America. And I would conclude by just making the point that there is one international diplomat who time and again is shown as having the objective and impartial stance to be able with some slender success at least to engage in this international diplomacy and that is the Secretary-General of the United Nations. And with all the best will in the world, the Secretary of State of the government of the United States, as indeed others such as the Foreign Minister of the Soviet Union, do not in the minds of the member states of the United Nations enjoy the same objectivity and impartiality as the U.N. Secretary-General does. So we would say in terms of the background that in one very real sense, by refusing to use that international machinery not only was the United Kingdom further humiliating the United Nations as the body which it helped to set up to avoid conflict, it was actually making war considerably more inevitable than it might have been.

Brigadier Michael Harbottle

I am addressing the subject of the peacekeeping aspect of the United Nations and the role that it could have played as I see it in the Falkland Islands Conflict had it been invited to do so. I think first of all I would like to define peacekeeping, because those of you who know the history of the U.N. and the U.N. Charter will know that peacekeeping operations as conducted by the U.N. in recent years do not conform with any article of the Charter, since the Charter when it was set down considered dealing with conflict only by enforcement means. Of course the peacekeeping operations have been quite the opposite. So let me just read to you the definition which is not in the Charter but is in the Peacekeepers' Handbook, which has been accepted by the United Nations as a training manual and a direction manual for U.N. operations and is used by something over 75 countries as the definitive training manual for U.N. operations. The definition reads:

"The prevention, containment, moderation, and termination of hostilities between or within states through the medium of a peaceful third party intervention organised and directed internationally, using multi-national forces of soldiers, police and civilians, to restore and maintain peace."

Now the Charter in two of its chapters, chapter six and seven, deals specifically with the methodology for maintenance of international peace and security. In chapter six they list a whole series of non-military actions such as embargoes, sanctions, economic, political and communication blockades and in chapter seven they devote themselves entirely to the use of force by the international body in order to, where necessary, maintain international peace and security. This chapter was implemented for the Korean War in the 1950s, but it only was used because the Soviet Union had withdrawn from the Security Council at that time and was not there to veto the decision. But it was quite evident, following the Korean War, that it was most unlikely that any U.N. force would ever be mounted in the same way again. It was from the Suez Campaign onwards that the new type of peacekeeping operation became the instrument of the United Nations in dealing with problems of international security and peace where the U.N. was invited to contribute. There is a proviso in the Charter in Article 2 which does allow for member states not, I repeat not, to bring matters to the United Nations when these issues and conflicts are in their view matters of domestic and not external issue. But the U.N. still maintains the right, under Section 39, that where international peace and security are threatened whatever the circumstances, they have the right to act even if it overrides Article 2.7. Now the principles of employment I think are also important if we are considering this problem. The first is "third party" in that the U.N. when it is introduced does not take sides in the dispute, it is there essentially as an impartial unit force or mission that is there to try and bring a solution by negotiation to the conflict existing between states or within states. The second is that the U.N. only operates in these circumstances when it is either asked to intervene, or a proposal to intervene is agreed to by the parties concerned. There is no imposition of forces under any circumstances under the current use of the peacekeeping procedure. In order that the impartiality can be strengthened, the principle is that the U.N. force does not use force in achieving the aims and objectives of its deployment. I think it might be interesting for you to understand that in Cyprus between 1964 and '68 when the U.N. brought the Cyprus conflict in military terms to an end, it did so without firing one single round of ammunition. And finally there is "self-defence" and that is only the use of your weapons if you are attacked, and I mention that because it has a correlation to Article 51 which H.M. Government used as a basis for actually operating in an enforcement manner in The Falklands. Article 51 says:

> "Nothing in the present Charter shall impair the inherent right of individual or collective self-defence if an armed attack occurs against a member of the United Nations."

Now what I challenge is that by using that and suggesting that self-defence was one of the major principles on which H.M. Government acted as it did in the Falkland Islands, I think one has to be very careful in assessing what that self-defence definition means. From the time that the attack took place on 2nd April, to the time that the first troops of the Task Force landed on Falkland shores was all of five weeks and in that period of time there had been negotiations to try and find a peaceful solution which is one of the provisos required in Article 51. So in my opinion it was a repossession, it was not in the true sense of the word a self-defence operation.

If I may I'd like to compare the kind of operations that the U.N. had conducted with those with which I was also involved in the years after the war, what we call the colonial wars, the internal security wars. I just want to deal briefly with this and I am prepared to substantiate my claim in any questioning afterwards, but so far as the internal security operations of post World War II, that is those of the United Kingdom, of France, of the Netherlands, of Portugal, of the United States in Vietnam and the U.S.S.R. in Afghanistan — if you look at the military results of all those internal security operations, they were militarily inconclusive and did not in any way achieve an end of those particular conflicts. Quite the contrary, the people who actually won were the people who were fighting for self-determination and who subsequently achieved their independence and were in fact headed in their governments by the people that we were fighting against. Now compared to that, the U.N. operations with far fewer soldiers, with far less active military enforcement action, did achieve in Cyprus in 1968 the role for which they were sent there to do. In the Congo in the 1960s they brought to an end a situation of which Monge Slim, the Foreign Minister of Tunisia, said, "Much controversy arose on the merits of such operations with many pros and cons but what can be asserted beyond any doubt is that the U.N. presence prevented the cold war from settling in the Congo, that the unity of the Congo was re-established thanks in large measure to the U.N.'s efforts, and that U.N. helped to avoid an impending chaos that threatened peace and security not only in the Congo but in the whole of the African continent." What the U.N. did during that operation was in fact to create a totally new administration from the old Belgian administration which had completely disappeared, and turned Congo into what was at least for a time, the most stable administrative government in the whole of central Africa. So that there are many incidences and examples of U.N. operations which, though not all successful, have in fact contributed and helped towards an end of the actual physical manifest violence of the conflict.

But I'd like to move specifically to two special operations of the United Nations which have a very great relevance to the Falkland Islands. The first was Indonesia in 1947 at a time when the Netherlands were in the process of giving up their colonial control over the Dutch East Indies to Indonesia and this had been fraught with difficulty and with conflict. In 1947 the United Nations established a Good Offices Commission which, working through the Consulates of certain nations in Jakarta in Indonesia and using the military missions as their observers on the spot, actually assisted the whole process of the decolonisation if you like of the Indonesian situation after the war; and in fact to give an example of what they achieved, they achieved a general cease fire, a delimitation of the status quo line of demilitarised zones, the evacuation of republican forces from the Netherlands' controlled areas and release of persons held as prisoners of war, and the evacuation of families of military personnel and their present welfare. Now those were fairly massive tasks for a small group of U.N. observers and that kind of Good Offices Commission to achieve, but it did achieve it.

In West Irian in 1962, again when there was the matter of the exchange of a Netherlands colonial rule for Indonesia, a U.N. temporary administration was set up which for eight months took over the running of that part of Papua and actually helped in the process of transition from the colonial rule to the hand over to Indonesia.

Now in both these examples I would point very firmly towards what might have been considered in the Falkland Islands. But in the Falklands we were faced with a negotiation situation which to my mind used wholely the wrong methods. I think it was on 7th April that Mr Haig was enrolled as negotiator and he worked for about five weeks, but he was working from a basis of inexperience as an international negotiator and he was politically involved as the United States was involved. But he was preferred to the Secretary-General who was an extremely experienced international negotiator and who had behind him the U.N. machinery. The second negotiation area was in fact the Peruvian President with Mr Haig working on an initiative which was aimed at bringing a solution to the problem without the need for military action. That, as you've heard from Malcolm, was sabotaged totally by the sinking of the Belgrano. But one of the things I think is interesting was that that initiative included a face-saving device which would have allowed the Argentinians to get off the hook. I think that it's interesting that at the very last moment when the agreement had been virtually put together, Costa Mendez is quoted both in Gavshon's book and in The Times report as saying to his staff, "We have an agreement, we can live with this." In other words a face-saving device had been found and that was very important in getting a solution to the problem because, as anybody knows who is in the negotiation field, you have to find a face-saving device to help the guilty party off the hook. But unfortunately H.M. Government was not interested in finding a face-saving device.

Just to conclude I will give simply the fact that my own personal initiative in this was that on 14th April, I submitted to Mr Douglas Hurd, then Minister in the Foreign Office, and to Mr Peter Archer in the House of Commons, a memorandum advising them of the two precedences of Indonesia and of West Irian as being models on which some kind of U.N. initiative could be developed which would suit the Falklands case and would provide an interim in which there could be a stabilization of the current situation, a withdrawal of both armed forces, the armed forces on the land and the Task Force off shore, so as to allow for a continuation of the Peruvian initiative which of course had come to a halt at the sinking of the Belgrano. More importantly there could also be a real positive U.N. initiative with the backing and at the request of H.M. Government. I also wrote to Mrs Thatcher on the 20th May, the day before the attack took place in San Carlos Bay, urging her to give the Secretary-General, the experienced man in negotiation, more time before any action was taken of a military nature to restore the situation. Unfortunately although the memo was in fact used by Mr Healey on 14th April in the House and it was discussed, neither of those initiatives I believe were ever contemplated as serious alternatives to the repossession by armed force by H.M. Government.

John Ferguson: I would like to ask Malcolm Harper a couple of questions, first in relation to H.M. Government's suggestion that the Russians might have used the veto. The Russians obviously used the veto a great deal in the early days of the U.N., would he indicate how much the Russians had used the veto in recent years, and secondly if they had used the veto could the United Nations still have acted?

Malcolm Harper: Well I haven't got the statistics in front of me of Soviet use of the veto in recent years but I can as a general guideline say that any member of the Security Council which has the right to veto uses it whenever its shorter term, more narrow nationalist interest is deemed to be threatened. Which is why I'm quite sure the United Kingdom vetoed the cease fire resolution of early June 1982 in the Security Council. The main areas in which now the Soviet Union threatens to, or uses, its veto are not least in connection with Afghanistan and to a certain extent Indo-China and particularly the Kampuchea problem. I will have to go away and come back tomorrow with the actual statistics if you would like them on the numbers of times they have used the veto.

In terms of a Soviet veto, had there been a follow-up resolution in the Security Council to 502, the United Nations could have sought to use what is called the Uniting for Peace Procedure. And the Uniting for Peace Procedure is available to try and get a veto in the Security Council overruled. If the General Assembly is not in session as it was not at the time of April 1982, then it is on paper and indeed to some extent in practice possible to summon a meeting, an extraordinary meeting of the General Assembly, not the Security Council, of the General Assembly within 24 or 36 hours of the Procedure being invoked, so long as support for the Procedure is given either by nine members of the Security Council or by a simple majority of member states in the General Assembly. And I believe I'm right in saying, but again I will have to check this out, that there is no right of veto within the Security Council at the time of the Uniting for Peace Procedure being invoked. So had the United Kingdom had its subsequent resolution vetoed by the Soviet Union, or China, or France, or America or all of them, the United Kingdom, had it had the political will to do so, could have invoked the Uniting for Peace Procedure and if the voting pattern on 502 was repeated they would within the Security Council have secured the requisite votes to get the Procedure invoked and then that could have gone on. Had there then in the General Assembly been a two-thirds majority in favour of the resolution which had been vetoed in the Security Council, the veto would have fallen.

John Ferguson: Thank you very much, that was a very useful clarification and the second question is again for clarification. I understand Malcolm Harper to be saying that while he would not assert that British action was illegal under Article 51, that Britain and the Argentine neither complied with Resolution 502 but that Britain really did miss a very big opportunity of putting the United Nations in the centre of things. And I notice that in the Minority Report 43 it is stated, 'In considering the prospect of the United Nations initiative the Prime Minister suggested that if Mr Haig could not pull off the settlement the Secretary-General could not either.' I understand Malcolm Harper to be challenging that sort of assertion.

Malcolm Harper: Yes, I am challenging that sort of assertion. I'm also to some extent saying I did not say that the British action was not illegal, I said its legality depended on whether you accepted that British sovereignty over the Islands was valid or invalid. If you accept the claim of sovereignty then you can argue, and I'm not taking issue with Michael Harbottle, you can argue that if that was British territory and British subjects living on it, and they came under armed attack by an external aggressor, then you had the right under Article 51 to use military force. But I would just in answering that like to read Article 51 because I think it's important that we should have the text of Article 51 on the record. Article 51 says, I quote:

'Nothing in the present Charter shall impair the inherent right of individual or collective self-defence if an armed attack occurs against a member of the United Nations...'

and I want you to bear in mind the next few words,

'until the Security Council has taken measures to maintain international peace and security. Measures taken by members in the exercise of this right of self-defence shall be immediately reported to the Security Council and shall not in any way affect the authority and responsibility of the Security Council under the present Charter to take at any time such action as it deems necessary in order to maintain or restore international peace and security.'

By not going back to the Security Council but by launching the Task Force on its journey south, I think we have to challenge how far the United Kingdom, even if you accept the argument of sovereignty, how far it actually fully stuck to the letter of Article 51 of the U.N. Charter. And if it did, and I think we need to be much clearer, what it did to stop the Task Force on its journey because the Security Council had taken the measures necessary to maintain international peace and security. By refusing to go back to the Security Council the United Kingdom actually made it impossible for the Security Council to fulfil its obligations in terms of Article 51 of the Charter.

Richard Baker: Does Malcolm Harper know whether the British Government or the Argentine Government or any other government, at any time proposed that the issue of the sovereignty of the Islands should be put to the International Court of Justice, or even to the Secretary-General at any time?

Malcolm Harper: Well there is evidence that at an early stage back in the 1940s Argentina had offered to submit the dispute on sovereignty to international arbitration. It was not taken up by the British and indeed it never got processed at that time. I have no recollection during the actual conflict from 2nd April onwards that either party was willing to submit to international jurisdiction through the International Court of Justice. And I think it certainly was highly doubtful that the Argentine Government at that stage would have been willing to, having committed itself in the way it had to an armed invasion; and the United Kingdom, although suddenly sovereignty had become unimpeachable, must have known in its heart of hearts that its claims were sufficiently dubious or controversial that it might have lost had it gone to international arbitration. So I believe I am correct in saying that there is no evidence that either party after 2nd April showed any willingness at any stage to submit the claim to arbitration.

Richard Baker: Is it an option?

Malcolm Harper: It's an option which remains open if both parties are willing to accept that it should go to international arbitration and that the decision of the International Court of Justice is binding on both parties.

Richard Baker: Is anything more known about what happened at Sir Anthony Parsons' dinner party?

Malcolm Harper: Well, I understand that by that time of course the great subject under discussion was the Peruvian Peace initiative and there seems to be a lot of confusion as to how much Mr Pym knew of the detail of the Peruvian Peace Initiative and opinions seem to be divided in British Government circles as to how much detail there was in the Peruvian Peace Initiative. I think it's in the Sunday Times book, there is the comment that Alexander Haig, earlier that day, had been sitting in his office in the United States and seemed to be having two telephones going simultaneously, one of them to Galtieri and the other to Belaunde Terry, and is reported to have made the comment at some stage during the discussions that they were actually down to the last one or two words to get agreement that this would be acceptable. Francis Pym subsequently appeared to deny all knowledge of a detailed discussion, although apparently, if the evidence is to be believed, he had been sitting for much of that day in Alexander Haig's office in the United States of America.

I think by the time that the dinner party took place, news of the sinking was coming through and even if the dinner party could have influenced events, the sinking of the Belgrano by that time had really scuppered any possibility of a diplomatic solution. But that said, I have to stress that Francis Pym did not have a mandate to see the Secretary-General so that the conversation over dinner was essentially an informal and not a formal part of the process of trying to find a diplomatic solution.

Michael Harbottle: Can I just add something to that and that is that while the sinking of the Belgrano did scupper the Peruvian Initiative, it would still have been perfectly possible, had there been the intent, with the end of the Haig initiative to have gone back to the United Nations and to have sought the good offices of the Secretary-General because, as we understand it, Anthony Parsons was working very hard with the Secretary-General right up to that moment and also with the representatives of the head of the Argentine mission. So that there was still an opportunity between then and 21st May when the troops were first landed on Carlos Bay. There were three weeks in which the Secretary-General could have made some progress and maybe deferred the whole action from the start.

Bill Hetherington (Peace Pledge Union): Would Malcolm Harper agree that a purely legalistic evaluation of claims to sovereignty of the Falkland Islands would be both inconclusive and irrelevant, and two, that both morally and within the United Nations self-determination should be the prime consideration, and three, that on that basis the Argentinian occupation was neo-colonialism but on the other hand there is a need for greater involvement by the Islanders in their own affairs?

Malcolm Harper: Yes, I think a narrowly legalistic definition is totally irrelevant, I think you have to take a much wider series of factors into account in determining the question of sovereignty. The question of self-determination is a highly complex one. Certainly within the United Nations the Decolonisation Committee has always stressed that self-determination for colonial peoples must be carried out with the utmost dexterity and speed and must always be in accordance with the expressed wishes of the people whose future is being determined by an end of colonialism.

The problem with the Falkland Islands is, was it a colony or was it an illegal occupation? Were the inhabitants of the Falkland Islands colonial subjects of the United Kingdom, or were they settlers on an area of land over which the United Kingdom did not have a valid claim? If it was a bona fide colonial structure then the procedure through United Nations auspices should be for the self-determination of the future of the Falkland Islands in accordance with the wishes of the inhabitants. If they were illegal occupants of a piece of land that the United Kingdom had no right to have possessed, then really they had no right to self-determination because the land is not theirs. And that is why the sovereignty issue remains the central issue and why this solution will never be satisfactorily resolved while we have one party to the dispute saying sovereignty is not available for discussion. If the Falkland Islanders are not there by legal right but by de facto occupation then you have a much more complex situation to deal with because they don't have the right of self-determination, they have the right to return to the United Kingdom. Until April 1982 something like 67% had the right of nationality, 33% didn't but suddenly they all became British, thanks to the House of Lords making amendments to the Nationality Act. That's their right to come back to the United Kingdom if they are illegal occupants of the Islands. If they are illegal occupants of the Islands but the legal owner of the Island, i.e. Argentina, says that they're quite happy for them to remain as inhabitants of the Islands under new ownership, then I think that the interests of the Islanders would obviously have to be taken into account in coming to a diplomatic solution of the crisis. And I stress the word *interests* because I do not believe that the Falkland Islanders have the right of veto until the sovereignty issue has been definitively resolved. Through ineptitude, and I stress the word ineptitude, by successive generations of British politicians of all parties, the interests and the rights of the Islanders to be involved in finding a solution has essentially become a veto by the Islanders. The Islanders have exercised that veto and any initiative towards a diplomatic solution has traditionally been blocked by the intransigence of the Islanders who have been given a level of power, that if my little community where I live in Oxfordshire was given we would be delighted, but we have no right to such power as parts of a wider community.

Nicholas Hyman: It seems to me that Article 51 does not apply to a disputed colonial territory, it applies to intrinsic sovereign territory which the Falkland Islands therefore was not. I won't go into the nationality question because you've already mentioned that these were not in fact British subjects...

Michael Harbottle: In reading Article 51 you also need to be aware of Article 2.7, because there is a relationship there as to what are the rights of member states: but I would have thought that Article 51 in this context was perfectly relevant. Surely the fundamental thing about Article 51 is that self-defence action is in conjunction with other actions by the Security Council. And I would have thought that by using Article 51 as an excuse, H.M. Government was virtually reading the first sentence and wasn't reading the whole of the Article. I would maintain that I think Article 51 is relevant but relevant to a point of view of actually being misinterpreted or misused by H.M. Government in order to justify an action that it subsequently took.

Malcolm Dando: I'm sorry we have to draw this session to a close. I think we should just ask our two speakers if they would like to say anything briefly?

Michael Harbottle: Yes, I would like to make just these very short comments. My conviction is that there was a peaceful solution there for the taking and in fact still is and the precedents that I quoted are models on which an interim U.N. third party initiative, or third party initiative of any kind could in fact be employed. And the second thing I would say is that I fear that a peaceful solution was never what H.M. Government wanted in the context of domestic political and party political prestige at that time. One thing is abundantly clear that in order to reach an agreement the United Kingdom and the Argentine have got to go back to the U.N. They are not going to solve this just between the two of them, they are going to have to use the machinery of the U.N. It's a great tragedy that that machinery was not used as much as it should have been at the time and bloodshed avoided. And I frankly rank the Falklands high on the list of the most unnecessary wars that have ever taken place.

II

The Slide into War

Tam Dalyell

Tam Dalyell

For over two years the Prime Minister in the House of Commons, the official account 'The Falkland Islands — The Lessons' paragraph 110 and the report by Sir John Fieldhouse, stated that our submarine the Conqueror had detected the Belgrano at 8 p.m. on Sunday the 2nd May; albeit during your trial, Clive, it became apparent that the official account had been altered behind Sir John Fieldhouse's back. That was what was said and held to — but it wasn't true. The truth was substantially and significantly different; that before 1600 hours on Friday the 30th April our submarine the Conqueror had picked up on her passive sonar first of all an oiler and then the Belgrano and her escorts the Hipolito Bouchard and the Piedra Buena. From 4 o'clock that South Atlantic afternoon at periscope depth the Conqueror closed in on the Belgrano and escorts. Throughout the forenoon of Saturday the 1st of May at a distance of 4,000 yards the Conqueror monitored the Belgrano and escorts refuelling at sea, during which time they were sitting-duck targets.

So one of the first questions that has to be asked is, why was it, when the 44-year old USS Phoenix, survivor of Pearl Harbour, for such the Belgrano was, was at the mercy of the Conqueror, why was the order, if the 44-year old Phoenix was such a threat to the modern ships of the British Task Force, why wasn't the order given there and then to sink it? No such order was given. From mid-day the Conqueror discreetly, at a distance of 10,000 yards, followed the Belgrano and escorts. If, panel, you think you need evidence for the 10,000 yards and many other of the detailed facts, I think I ought to tell you that from a very early stage there was put into my possession the authentic diary, not the log book, but the authentic diary of the Supplies Officer of the Conqueror. For a long time I kept it very secret for obvious reasons, but it is now well known that Lieutenant Narendra Sethia's diary contained wholly accurate facts.

At 7 minutes past 8 on that Saturday evening, 1 May, an order went out from the Operational Commander, Admiral Allara, on board The 25 de Mayo, the old HMS Venerable, ordering the

Argentine Surface Group back to Staten Island. That order was
confirmed by the Naval Command in Buenos Aires at 1.19 a.m.
the following morning. Both these orders are reprinted in Arthur
Gavshon's book that you have, and I think he would allow me to
say that one of the reasons why some of us were able to persuade
him to write the book, was that in 30 years as head of the
Associated Press of America office in London he had not known
so many mutually contradictory explanations given by a British
Government on sensitive issues. Both these orders, like most other
orders, were intercepted, actually by the AD 470 high frequency
Marconi transceiver equipment on board the Task Force; flashed
back to Ascension Island and then to GCHQ at Cheltenham where
they were decrypted in a minute to a minute and a half — not very
difficult at the best of times, even easier when those who had
devised the orders had been trained by us at Portsmouth shortly
before.

So, the question arises, why was it that at mid-day, lunchtime at
Chequers, the British Prime Minister, together with Lord Lewin,
gave an order which was more likely in those waters at that time
of year, to mean a thousand lives lost, a thousand sailors drowned,
rather than the 368 who actually perished? It is my belief, based
on sources that I'm not prepared even at this stage to reveal, that
it was not the responsibility of Naval Command at Northwood. I
say to you that before he left Northwood there was a consensus
of opinion that Lord Lewin knew about, that it would be more
dangerous rather than less dangerous for our Task Force to have
a sinking of the Belgrano, because the threat rightly perceived by
the professional naval command at Northwood, was that the threat
came from land-based aircraft and not from the six inch guns,
range 13 miles, on the 44-year old cruiser. So it's no good saying
that this was simply the fault of the Navy. It was a conscious
political decision of the Prime Minister. And why? Because that
Saturday evening and certainly Sunday morning she knew
something else: that was, as Michael Harbottle has outlined, the
government of Peru was putting forward proposals to the United
States that the United Nations, the Organisation of American
States, our European partners and many others, would expect us
to accept. Though, of course, had the Prime Minister accepted
them she would have been deprived of the military victory that the
Falklands war was all about from a very early stage.

I have to say to the panel that I gave evidence for an hour and
twenty-five minutes to Lord Franks and his committee and you
will see, paragraphs 146 to 156, that on 3rd March Ambassador
Anthony Williams in Buenos Aires was warning of a likely attack
on the Falklands. Franks records that on the 7th March in her own

handwriting Mrs Thatcher wrote in the margin of the Ambassador's despatch "We must have contingency plans." I'm not here to namedrop but I'm told by Lord Sherfield, who as Sir Roger Makins was head of the Treasury, Ambassador to Washington and much else, by Lord Brimelow, former Permanent Under Secretary at the Foreign Office and by Lord Hunt a former Cabinet Secretary, that a Prime Ministerial note in the margin of an Ambassador's report that has been deemed sufficiently important to put in the Prime Ministerial red box has the force of a Cabinet Minute. So it wasn't in fact some off-the-cuff comment which we were dealing with, this was a very forceful indication. What Mrs Thatcher knew was that the Peruvians were putting forward these peace proposals, and I have to report to the panel and to the audience, that at my own expense — I say this because it has been said that I'm the creature of this Latin American government or that — on an academic fare I went to Peru, spent an hour and 35 minutes with Belaunde Terry and he explained in detail in his office in Lima what had happened: that, first of all, it was to be Peruvian and American troops. The Americans weren't acceptable to the Argentines, the Peruvians weren't acceptable to us, and therefore arrangements were being made for Mexican, West German and Canadian troops. Part of the bargain was that the Argentine forces should get off the Falkland Islands forthwith and that the Task Force would either halt or turn round. Belaunde in a very human way explained to me that he'd been extremely close to the the British Ambassador Charles Wallace because Charles Wallace's wife was Spanish and their family had been kind to the Belaunde Terrys when they had been exiled during the first military government of Peru, to Spain. It was that kind of close relationship. He said to me, "I know that your government and your Prime Minister knew exactly was I was doing." And he said, "One day there will be the documentary evidence."

Now I believe that somewhere that documentary evidence does exist but Peru has many problems, they don't want gratuitous trouble with any British Government. They have great debt problems even with the successor government of Garcia with the Luminoso and other problems. And I can understand it that they don't want to produce documents that would be greatly embarrassing, not only to British Governments, but to themselves. But I believe that such documentation exists.

I sat in the house of Manuel Ulloa, the chairman of the Development Committee of the World Bank, the Prime Minister of Peru at the time, who said to me, "Look, what do you take us for? We were negotiators and to be negotiators you have to be in touch with both sides. I know," he said — and there were no language difficulties, his daily reading was the Wall Street Journal and nor was he of my general political outlook — he said, "I know that through Lord Hugh Thomas and others, that your Government and your Prime Minister knew precisely what we were doing that Saturday and Sunday."

I talked to Oscar Mauortua the head of Belaunde's office, two years at Pembroke College Oxford, so therefore no language difficulties again. He said, "Look, you have to understand that the whole government of Peru came to a halt that weekend, we were so concerned." And what Oscar Mauortua said was, "We were concerned both at the Task Force coming and the prospect of battle and the fact that your Task Force we knew was bringing nuclear weapons which was an infringement of Protocol One of the Treaty of Tlatelolco which you yourselves had signed." Eric Ogden will remind us that the Argentines hadn't signed it. The same information was given in public by Arias Stella on Panorama.

But of course it is a brutal truth that Peruvian evidence will not be sufficient and therefore we turn to North America and Malcolm Harper made reference to Alexander Haig. Now in Haig's memoirs (and part of them have been changed, but this has not been changed) "Acceptance," he said, "was gained in principle from both parties." Now why should Mrs Thatcher's admirer Haig say this unless he believed it to be true, supported by Woody Goldberg his assistant, supported by Dean Fisher the Assistant Secretary for Public Affairs, the official spokesman of the State Department at the time, and indeed by other Americans?

But we can come this side of the Atlantic because it's on the record, again on Panorama. Pressed by Emery, Mr Parkinson let the cat out of the bag. "Yes," he said, "we knew all about peace proposals that Sunday morning, primarily those of President Belaunde." And when I had the opportunity of pressing Cranley Onslow, then Minister of State at the Foreign Office, on the Brass Tacks programme, he said, "Well the Foreign Office knew all about the peace proposals on the Sunday morning."

Now I put it to the panel: if the Foreign Office knew, didn't Downing Street know and if Mr Parkinson knew, didn't Mrs Thatcher know? Was there, to use the lingo of Westlands which in some ways is an action reply of the Belgrano, the same withholding of information from ministers entitled to know, the same tampering with official documents, the same lying to the House of Commons? To use the language of Westlands, was there some 'misunderstanding'?

For the purposes of a serious tribunal like this, one has to be extremely careful and not over-exaggerate the case. It is conceivable that reasonable people would think that there was no possibility of the Peruvian proposals being accepted by the Argentines. All I can say is that the internal evidence and the evidence from the United States is that shortly before he was called out to be told that his ship had been sunk, that the hardline Admiral Anaya was about to sign and the independent witnesses here, neither of whom I had talked to, this morning, quite independently, said the same thing about the Junta and I have every belief that that is true. Reasonable people could also say that the Peruvian proposals did not form the basis for a long-term settlement which General Haig described as "Two bald men fighting over a comb." But you see, what other kind of settlement nearly as advantageous to our country is there? And we speak in a week, and it's not the business in my opening at any rate to comment on this, we speak in a week where the situation could fester and become awful again. No long term military solution to be had. Where reasonable people cannot differ is that when Mrs Thatcher says that no news of the Peruvian proposals reached London until 3 hours after the Belgrano was sunk (or more precisely in answer to the Shadow Cabinet, written on behalf of the Shadow Cabinet by Denzil Davies the spokesman) she said, "The first indication of the Peruvian proposals reached London at 11.15 p.m. on Sunday 2nd May." That is not true. Michael Harbottle used the word 'sabotage'. I haven't used that particular word before but I think it is a very apt description of the situation.

Now you asked me some precise questions, first of all about the Belgrano itself. From the 2nd April I had opposed the sending of the Task Force, as you said in your Introduction and on 3rd April, I had pleaded to speak, to put a dissenter's point of view. But Mr Speaker, George Thomas, to his eternal discredit, would have none of it. Not because he didn't call Tam Dalyell, but because he didn't call any of the more vociferous dissenters. We now know from his memoirs why: because he took a view of the national interest, that the Prime Minister had to be supported. The memoirs of George Thomas really are very revealing. On 4th April I made a statement fully carried in the heavy newspapers, that the sending of the Task Force was the most illconceived expedition to leave these shores since the Duke of Buckingham had left for La Rochelle in 1627, and daily opposed the sending of the Task Force. However I ought to tell the panel that I did not criticize the sinking of the Belgrano on the 4th May. It happened on the 2nd of May. On the 4th of May the House of Commons had its first opportunity and I asked whether it was done with the authority of the Prime Minister. "Yes," came the answer. "full political control." And because war is very nasty and because, like my colleagues, I believed the explanation that John Nott had given

that this was some submarine commander acting fast to protect
the Task Force, because after all the Belgrano was converging on
the Task Force, that war is very unpleasant, but this was for
protection of British servicemen. And that was what I accepted
as gospel until July 1982 when I read on page 7 of The Scotsman
newspaper an artless article by a reputable journalist Eric
Mackenzie who'd been sent to welcome home the Conqueror to
Faslane and had asked a question that flowed logically from what
Nott had said in the Commons. "Why, Commander Wreford-
Brown, did you sink the Belgrano?" And his answer was very
revealing. "Oh," he said, "I didn't sink the Belgrano off my own
bat. I wouldn't do a thing like that. I'm a first-time submarine
commander. I did it," he said, "on orders from Northwood." Now
this was totally different from what Parliament, press and the
people had been told. And I put it to the panel that it's the old
question of small inconsistencies being part of larger
inconsistencies, small lies being part of larger lies.

Now if in August or September or October 1982, the
Government had made anything like a clean breast of it and said,
"Look we had to enter into some deception, it was war, the real
position is..." Instead of it we got a whole series of false
statements: that they had to do it because of the Burdwood Bank,
and when I went to the briefing of the Ministry of Defence, Sir
Sandy Woodward said, "Well, we had to do it urgently because"
and this was the answer to parliamentary questions) "otherwise
we'd have lost the Belgrano in going over the Burdwood Bank."
Now when one looked at the coordinates, she'd been and was
going and was known to be going nowhere near the Burdwood
Bank. Anyhow these waters are well charted — average depth of
Burdwood Bank 90 fathoms, minimum depth 25 fathoms. These
SSNs are built with the capacity to operate in the Baltic which is
a shallow sea and it just, to anybody who knew the details of it
and made enquiries, just did not ring true.

Now let me say one thing on mobilisation. You see, if you look
at the Hansard carefully for the 3rd April (and often things are
done in annoyance) John Nott was interrupted by Julian Amery.
Now Mr Amery's politics are not mine but on this kind of issue
he's a very serious member of the House of Commons and has a
long history of membership of the House of Commons and Nott
snapped back at him, "We were not unprepared, preparations had
been going on for weeks." It's there in the Hansard of the 3rd
April and I believe it to be true. This was in a sense the Argentines
being lured on to the punch. I'm not saying that she put up Galtieri
to do this in the first place, what I am saying is that it was very
definitely in the political interest of a Prime Minister, lower in the

opinion polls than any Prime Minister had been since opinion polls started, at that time, to let it run.

You ask me about Francis Pym. I believe that Francis Pym was a basically honourable man. I believe that, like Lord Whitelaw, also a holder of the Military Cross, he knew what war was about and was going to Washington in the belief that he would be able to do something about it. I didn't know until this morning what Malcolm Harper said about having not fixed up an official meeting with Perez de Cuellar, that this was all done through Anthony Parsons and that is certainly a new fact. But you see, what is impossible to swallow about the Pym mission is, first of all, that he didn't contact the Americans on arrival because he arrived by Concorde; secondly, that throughout the morning he was with General Haig, he then went back to the embassy and a phone call came through from Haig emphasising the importance of the Peruvian proposals, wanting to speak to Francis Pym. But he didn't have time to speak to Haig. For why? He had a plane to catch! A plane to where? To New York. Now services in high summer between Washington and New York aren't exactly infrequent and as we heard this morning, this was a somewhat late engagement. The truth as I believe it was that he didn't want to be in the position of accepting the phone call. Had he done so, he would either have been in the position of deceiving the Americans — and if he deceived the Americans how could he remain a Foreign Secretary dealing with our closest ally? — or, he would have had to let the cat out of the bag, that he had been told by London that something was afoot (not necessarily that the Belgrano was going to be sunk). So, in one very real sense, the torpedo was not only fired at the Argentines, but I believe in one sense it was fired at Francis Pym, because the political situation was such that had anything gone wrong, Francis Pym, moved to the Foreign Office very much against the Prime Minister's wishes, would have certainly gone from the Foreign Office to 10 Downing Street.

I believe, panel, that the events of 1982 unfinished, reflect maximum discredit on those who made the key decisions. If I seem to be personal to the Prime Minister, it's not a blanket attack on my political opponents, not the Conservative Party, not even the Cabinet, because it's a known fact, unchallenged, that for 33 days as between April 2nd and May 5th Mrs Thatcher never called together her full cabinet to discuss the conduct of the Falklands War. If I seem to be very personal it's because the Falklands War was very personal to the British Prime Minister.

John Ferguson: I've been very impressed by what we've heard, very frank and open statements. One's problem is that there is reference to evidence, that in some ways runs counter to the evidence which the Foreign Affairs Committee had before them. I wonder whether Mr Dalyell would like to comment on particularly the evidence of Charles Wallace? Is it his view that Charles Wallace didn't really have any serious knowledge of what was going on, because in his evidence to the committee he suggests that he didn't have anything which he could seriously communicate with the Government?

Tam Dalyell: I'm not going to get up in public and accuse a civil servant of lying. All I said to you was that I believe that Charles Wallace was put in an impossible position. I was at that hearing. I'm not sneering at him, he has a career and it's a very, very impossible position for a civil servant to be put in, because had Charles Wallace said anything different he might have landed up in the position of Clive Ponting. I would rather leave it at that but I believe that when the full story comes to be told Charles Wallace's very personal dilemma in an impossible situation will be revealed, and not to his discredit. I'm not going to attack him.

John Ferguson: Thank you for that. I wonder whether again Dalyell would like to comment on one or two items which were in the Prologue, for example the involvement of General Alexander Haig as mediator, on which I don't think he actually said anything.

Tam Dalyell: Well a good deal has been said this morning by Malcolm Harper about Haig and I would agree very strongly with Malcolm Harper that it would have been better had the United Nations been involved. On Haig, I repeat what Haig said in his own memoirs, that acceptance was gained in principle from both parties. Now if he hadn't meant that why did he not change it, because a number of other things in the memoirs were changed?

Richard Baker: There are two questions, Chairman. I think in the beginning were one or more ships carrying nuclear weapons, can you enlarge on this?

Tam Dalyell: Yes. Would the panel mind if I enlarged on this at some length? From Operation Springtrain from Gibraltar on the Royal Fleet Auxiliary Fort Austin there went nuclear depth charges. The evidence for this can be found from the National Union of Seamen, Jim Jolly or Jim Jump or Jim Slater, their former General Secretary, who got it from a man called Michael Flockhart who was the shop steward, so to speak, of the National Union of Seamen onboard the Royal Fleet Auxiliary Fort Austin. And in those moving Tinker diaries you'll see that the young Lieutenant, shortly to be killed, on the Glamorgan went aboard the Fort Austin and wrote in his diary that he was amazed to see dummy nuclear weapons. Well of course there were dummy nuclear weapons because they had to have dummies for drill purposes between helicopter and ships.

From Southampton, Portsmouth and Devonport we have the evidence of Sir Ronald Mason now Professor of Chemistry at the University of Sussex, then Chief Scientist at the Ministry of Defence, that he tried very hard indeed to get nuclear weapons taken off in the Channel, some were brought back and others weren't. But of course there is worse: that the diver who went down into the tomb of the Coventry and looked at equipment emanating radio-nucleides, wasn't searching for codebooks as the press said, and he was awarded the Queen's Gallantry medal for his work in looking for nuclear weapons that had gone down with the Coventry.

Dr Paul Rogers of the University of Bradford has outlined at length in print recently in the New Statesman, and I think you'd better ask Dr Rogers directly about this, the circumstances in which a Polaris submarine went 21 degrees west, 12 degrees south out of range of the Soviet Union and in range of Argentina. I have it from Professor John Ericson, professor of Defence Studies in Edinburgh that it would be totally frivolous to send a Polaris submarine to that area simply for the use of her torpedo tubes. That would be a very frivolous thing to do. Dr Rogers will outline, if you ask him, at length, the whole question of how the Conqueror returned so short of food because the other submarines were protecting the Polaris submarine and couldn't be deployed for normal SSN duties.

Richard Baker: Could I ask whether Professor John Ericson made these views public or is this the first time?

Tam Dalyell: Professor Ericson has been quite open about it and so I gather has Sir Ronald Mason.

Richard Baker: It's on the record somewhere then?

Tam Dalyell: I think it would be a very good thing for the tribunal to contact Sir Ronald Mason himself at Sussex.

Richard Baker: The only other question I have is a rather general one about whether the diary gives details of messages going back and forth between various places and Number 10 and so on; and if you agree that whether or not information or bits of paper reached the Prime Minister or other ministers, the Prime Minister and the Cabinet are not only politically and actually responsible for all these goings on described, and if they didn't know they ought to have known. Even if the statements you've made about messages between Number 10 were contradictory, the responsibility remains, does it not, with the government just as the commander of the submarine for...

Tam Dalyell: Yes, you see there is a high degree of personal responsibility... in no sense can this Prime Minister say as Macmillan said in a different context, "No one told me." Because it was quite clear that it was the War Cabinet who were running things and indeed, inside the War Cabinet itself it was the sort of troika of Mrs Thatcher, Parkinson and Lewin involved, and how much Pym and Whitelaw were told is open to considerable question.

Malcolm Dando: Can I just follow that up with a short question before you answer questions from the floor? I understand there was a thing called the 'Mandarin's Committee' which processed officially ... and that this did not meet before...

Tam Dalyell: The Mandarin's Committee was bypassed, and two of the questions that you've asked me should in all conscience have been answered by Government following the Select Committee Report, because the Select Committee Report, and I gather that Mr Mikardo is to be one of your witnesses later on, did ask 30 questions. Now what happened briefly is that the Foreign Affairs Select Committee Report was published at the very fag-end of the last moment of the 1985 session. And it still has not been debated in the House of Commons. Lo and behold — on Westlands, the Select Committee Report was published on the penultimate day of the last session, and therefore there was the whole summer recess before there could be any proper discussion. Though I had a debate the following day, which may be known to the panel, where there was a complete bromide on answers, this was on Westlands, which can't directly concern you. But this is the political tactic of using time so that other events overtake these matters. Now you could well ask me as to why the opposition didn't press more strongly that these matters should be investigated. And if I were so asked I would give you a rather candid answer.

Richard Baker: Mr Dalyell mentioned that Pym and Whitelaw were not informed, I take it that he would accept that they as Cabinet ministers were responsible for what went on, whether or not they were informed. The Cabinet were surely responsible for all that was going on, were they not?

Tam Dalyell: Yes. My criticism of this Cabinet is that they didn't confront their Prime Minister and ask what on earth she was doing and my criticism is one frankly of fecklessness, because I would hope that any member of a British Cabinet in such a situation would demand to know that which was being done in their name; because otherwise the whole question of ministerial responsibility and Cabinet government breaks down.

Helen Trask (C.D.I.O.): I understand that the Falkland Islands was, and is, strategically important to Britain as a gateway to the

Antarctic. How important do you think this factor was in deciding to take over these islands by force?

Tam Dalyell: I don't want in any way to snub Helen and you'll acquit me of frivolity but the Falkland Islands do have great strategic importance and that's for Gentoo Penguins. I honestly think that there is no, in this day and age, (whatever was the position in 1914 with coley) strategic importance at all on a global basis. There is of course the related question of Antarctica but anything that is done for the exploitation of Antarctica must surely be done with agreement of our co-signatories to the Antarctic Treaty who are the Americans, the Russians, the West Germans, the Chileans, the Argentines, not to mention easy people like the French. So we really have to accept that anything in Antarctica must be done by the nations of the world who are signatories to the Antarctic Treaty. Now if you ask me about economic wealth, none of us know whether there are significant hydro-carbon deposits in the Malvinas Trench but I live in and represent a constituency, where many of my constituents work on North Sea oil rigs and it's difficult enough to win oil (as we were tragically reminded yesterday in Shetland), from the North Sea even with the backup facilities of Methil and Aberdeen, Solom Voe and Stavanger on the other side. How much more difficult to win oil from the Furious Fifties or the Roaring Forties without the whole engineering backup which would have to come from the Chilean and the Argentine mainland! So without agreement with Argentina not a drop of oil would be won.

Audrey Smith: With regard to size of arsenal of nuclear weapons, are you sure these all exist or is it a gigantic con trick to frighten the world and its people?

Tam Dalyell: I wish it was a con trick, but unfortunately they do exist and you see what we're talking about is the possibility of a Russian plus in the South Atlantic. Now it would be an insult to you, and I would never ever I hope do this, to raise bogies in which I didn't really believe but you see there really was in the House of Commons at the time, a substantial number of MPs who said if the Argentines don't get off we really must use our nuclear capability, albeit that we promised absolutely solemnly that we would never use or even threaten a non-nuclear power. If you think this is fanciful go back to Tinker's book because it was never thought to be published, but there it is in print: "Blank, blank suggested that we should drop a 'big white job', (that's the naval slang for a Polaris missile), on Buenos Aires, thank God he's not in command." Now why should the young Lieutenant in what he believed to be a document which would never be published, write that, unless he believed it to be true? But Paul Rogers will expand on a subject in which has has particular expertise.

Diana Gould: The Haig plan was thrown out by Argentina on April 29th. On April 30th the United States 'tilted' in our favour. Do you think this fact would have made Galtieri more likely to accept the Peruvian plan on 2nd May?

Tam Dalyell: My judgement is not only Galtieri but the other Argentines and it's also the view of Guillermo Makin and other experts in the field. But you see a partial answer to you, was the state of the Prime Minister's mind on this. Now I have to say to the meeting that I think I was the only Labour MP actually to go and see Mrs Thatcher, at the time. And can we go 8 days earlier?

On 20th April Roy Jenkins (then the newly elected member for the Hillhead division of Glasgow) asked, "The Falklands is so serious can the Party leaders," of which he was then one, "come and see you?"

"Oh yes," said the Prime Minister, "of course," and added, "I will see any member of Parliament who wishes to see me about this."

So I thought, having read it the following morning and checked what she'd actually said, that I would put in a request to go, giving a number of reasons, partly that I'd sat in in the 1970s at the request of Jim Callaghan who was then Foreign Secretary, and I was chairman of the Labour Party Foreign Affairs Group on the Falkland Islands seminars in the Foreign Office, where they were represented by Mr Leolin Price QC and I thought that they were asking for very unreal objectives. So I knew something of the background. I also had an interest in military technology and knew that the Argentines were formidably armed, and I had led the Parliamentary delegation to Brazil and knew something of South America and that they were likely to fight, and so I gave a whole number of reasons. Now in fairness, she saw me at half past nine that night in her room in the company of Ian Gow and it started off on a perfectly friendly basis, because I had been parliamentary private secretary to the late Dick Crossman and he'd worked closely with Charlie Pannell. Charlie Pannell's PPS, this is rather complicated, was Terry Boston, now Lord Boston of Faversham, who'd gone off to Australia because his wife was Australian and there was illness in the family, and so I stepped in and did his job for him for a bit. Charlie Pannell's pair was Margaret Thatcher, so I knew her of old.

I started off by saying, "It's very good of you Margaret to see me."

"Oh," she said, "I'm always happy to see the awkward squad."

I then said that one of my earliest childhood memories had been the distress of my parents when they'd heard that the Prince of

Wales and the Repulse had gone down off Malaya and this was all about landbased aircraft and capital ships.

"Oh Yes," she said, didn't I know that one of her closest advisers, was Sir Henry Leach, who was the son of the captain of the Prince of Wales? Well then the argument got tougher and tougher and I went back to my colleagues and said, "Look, in the absence of the humiliation of Argentina she really wants a fight."

Now that's not just Tam Dalyell's opinion as of the 21st April, because if you read Sara Keays' book (and actually I'm totally uninterested in petty scandal of any kind, I'm not interested in people's private lives, I'm extremely interested in their public actions) what Sara Keays reveals is that Parkinson had come back to her on the 18th April, one of the few times he'd criticized the Prime Minister, and said that it was inevitably going to be war. Now all I invoke Miss Keays for is to back up my statement that she'd made up her mind on war long, long before 29th April or indeed, let alone when she sent Francis Pym on what the House of Commons believed was a peace mission to Washington.

Jean Woolf: In Steve Berkoff's play 'Sink the Belgrano!' he very clearly implies that Francis Pym actually picked up the telephone, talked to Mrs Thatcher and was told to carry on with the peace plan. Have we any further evidence since your book that Pym actually had direct directions from Mrs Thatcher or is that merely the ...?

Tam Dalyell: Well I have to give you the straight answer, that as far as I know that is still unproven that there was direct conversation. I would think it extremely strange if either there was not direct conversation or through the Permanent Secretary of the Foreign Office who was at that time Sir Anthony Acland. You refer to Steve Berkoff's play. I don't want to be prim about it, but I have not gone to see the play or any other work of fiction on the Belgrano because I of all people must not get fact confused with fiction. Now I'm not saying that he was right or wrong to have written it, all I'm saying is that I personally have had nothing to do with it, have not gone to see the play, nor any plays on Hilda Murrell for the reason that I can't get confused in my mind fact and fiction.

Nicholas Hyman: Do you believe that Margaret Thatcher personally ordered the sinking of the Belgrano and as a supplementary, do you also believe that she, while visiting the naval headquarters, shocked some people by having enthusiasm for 'the kill'?

Tam Dalyell: I do believe but I can't prove it, that she was often at Northwood. I mean I know she was there from time to time, whether she was there during the actual sinking is something which will never be known. There are people who I trust who are quite sure that she was, but I have no actual proof and therefore I've got to be extremely careful on this. But the whole attitude, displayed by the Prime Minister when she went to address the Conservative Party at Cheltenham racecourse, really revealed a situation where, I don't think it's unfair to say, she seemed to glory in war. Certainly on a radio broadcast that she did on the 14th of May in Scotland, when she was visiting the Conservative Party Conference she said, and I can't remember the words accurately at this stage, but to the effect that throughout her political life she'd had to deal with the social services and with education, but here it was thrilling because it was a matter of right and wrong. And indeed a recording of that broadcast certainly exists in IRN.

Questioner from floor: Have you wished that you had resigned from the Labour Party...

Tam Dalyell: No, because I would never resign from the Labour Party. But I think there's a very clear question that has to be answered and that is the attitude of the Labour Party at the time. I think it's much better to be very candid about it. On the 2nd of April John Silkin who was then Shadow Defence Spokesman was cornered by Widlake into saying that the Labour Party in certain circumstances would use force. Now I was so concerned about this that I rang up, couldn't get through to John Silkin, got through to Anne Carlton who was his assistant, and she said, "Look I'll find out about the position." Two hours later she rang back and said it was all right, it was all a misunderstanding, the Party was committed to no such thing.

I was in a meeting in my constituency that night, went back and Kathleen my wife said, "Look, I've heard the ten o'clock news and it's not all right." So I got the early shuttle to London, did what I've never done before or since, got a taxi in from London airport to the House of Commons, in order to see Michael Foot. Forgive me for the length of this but it's relevant to the implication of your question.

When I saw Michael Foot I said to him, "Look, as your science spokesman I must tell you that these people are formidably armed and secondly, with Latin American experience, that they will fight."

His reply was not dishonourable. What he said was, "You don't understand fascism sufficiently."

And you see for Michael Foot who'd come to prominence by that pamphlet 'Guilty Men', the attack on Sir Samuel Hoare and other appeasers, Leopaldo Galtieri was a sort of reincarnation of Benito Mussolini and the threat had to be met and this was the time to stand up against fascism. And also much of the party felt very strongly on the issue of human rights, people like Stan Newens, with impeccable socialist credentials. It then happened on that Saturday morning that Michael Foot made a speech where he departed from his notes and went over the top. Because it was a truncated debate, Silkin wound up before any of us had had an opportunity to speak and he made an even sillier speech. From that moment the Labour Party was on a motorway from which there was no easy exit. It was a tiger that you couldn't dismount from, it was a moving staircase that you couldn't get off.

From then on it was very difficult as the Task Force headed south. But most people believed that it would never come to a fight, that the Americans would sort it out, that the United Nations would sort it out, that our European partners would sort it out, that the Organisation of American States would sort it out, that Mr Micawber would turn up, that something would happen. But the bulk never believed that the Task Force would actually get much beyond the Western Approaches. I happened to make a different judgement. And there was something else. There was the view of Jim Callaghan and a number of others that the Labour Party had been thought to be insufficiently patriotic at the time of Suez, and because we were perceived to be insufficiently patriotic, then we lost the 1959 general election. Therefore they said, allow the Task Force to proceed, back our boys, it'll be sorted out don't worry, and the Conservatives will land in a mess of their own.

Now I say to you quite openly, that those people who put short-term political expediency, electoral expediency before the principles in which they really believe, tend to get their come-uppance. I admit to you and give that to you quite openly. If you say to me, why don't I leave the Labour Party on this, the truth is that I had enormous support from the Labour Party in the country and have continued to have from a very early stage when incidentally my views were extremely unpopular. No difficulty for me because I'm a Scot, and do you know from my 95,000 constituents how many letters of complaint there were? Precisely four, and one was a poem from the local baker who was more concerned with his poetry than any serious criticism. The problems came from the south of England, this city, Birmingham and the Home Counties and the socialist colleagues who stood up in the south of England were infinitely braver than I was. Now, the Party was marvellous and throughout the difficult times I got such support from the Labour Party that I will for ever be proud to be a member of that Party.

Nicholas Russell: Do you think that the nuclear weapons would have been used if Britain failed in the conventional war? If so, would the targets have been and how many weapons would have been used?

Tam Dalyell: The story I believe is this, that in the ugly period between the loss of the Sheffield and the landing at San Carlos, high naval persons went to the Prime Minister and said, "Look, the situation is such that if we lose a major unit, the Canberra, the Invincible or the Hermes, the task which you have given us, to repossess the Falkland Islands, cannot be implemented."

She replied, "Defeat is unthinkable."

They said, "But you must understand the logistics of it, we can't do it if we lose a major unit."

"In which case," I believe that she replied, "we must teach them a lesson."

And teaching them a lesson was dropping a nuclear missile on the Argentine city of Cordoba, roughly the equivalent of the Aldershot area. That's what I believe took place, and certainly there were many Conservative MPs who — in my opinion, frivolous to the point of unbelief — were advocating nuclear weapons unless the Argentine forces withdrew. I believe that politicians faced with humiliation and defeat will do very irrational things and that's why the episode of the Falklands convinced me to become a member of Campaign for Nuclear Disarmament.

Wade Tidbury (a member of the Task Force): I would like to ask Tam Dalyell if he was aware of the fuss which went on throughout the fleet with the officers and the like, upon the sinking of the Sheffield, to the exact position being recorded upon the computers in the operations room of every ship, for the exact position of the ship in her death throes. Was he aware of that?

Tam Dalyell: No. Not fully, though I have talked to some of the crew members of the Sheffield and am rather sorry for the captain of the Sheffield, not because he didn't get an honour, but because of the imputations that have been made about him professionally, and it may well have been that the Sheffield was placed in a situation that it never ought to have been placed in. I won't go into the detailed questions of whether the Exocet should or should not have been picked up and whether it was identified as a friendly weapon or not. My comment to you is that much of the information has come to me, not because of the colour of my politics but from those on the Task Force who believe that their lives were risked, that some of their friends didn't come back, and others came back maimed, not for the national interests of Britain but for the political interests of the British Prime Minister. A very different story.

I give you my word of honour that not knowingly has a word of criticism of British servicemen escaped my lips, other than of Lord

Lewin, and then in his capacity as a member of the War Cabinet and not as an Admiral of the Fleet. Much of the information has come to me from servicemen who are extremely upset about what they were asked to do. People who would certainly fight in any just war for this country. But then you see we have to define a just war. And I go back to the old business of St Augustine and St Thomas Aquinas, that to have a just war every effort must be made to avoid the war. The Aquinas/Augustine definition has not been satisfied in this case.

But as to servicemen themselves, I have a history of being deeply concerned and interested in the Services as a Member of Parliament for 24 years and certainly I'm not going to be snide or unfair to British servicemen. If I can just add one thing, I did not sign, and a lot of my friends thought I should have done and should have been active about it, an enquiry into Goose Green and the Welsh Guards and all that; because there may have been mistakes but it's no part of my case to start undermining the confidence of, and blaming some unfortunate officers in the Welsh Guards who must have it on their conscience for the rest of their lives. Equally as I talk Mrs Cockton, the mother of the co-pilot of the helicopter that was shot down by HMS Cardiff, that I had known about it for some months for certain, that is in the Sethia Diaries, but it was no part of my case to give pain either to the crew of the Cardiff, who must be full of remorse, or to the crew of the helicopter relatives who must be saddened beyond belief that they had been shot down by one of our own weapons. Mrs Cockton thought that I ought to have been franker about it and maybe she was right but as far as I was concerned, this kind of agony was no part of the case that I'd been putting forward. Now I've tried to answer your question. You come back because it may be important information.

Wade Tidbury: Well, the first thing I'm talking about, on the ship that I was serving on, HMS Alacrity, revolved around officers shouting for charts and making sure that the computers actually recorded the exact position without any question. I think this was because of a nuclear weapon, nuclear depth charge on the Sheffield. I can't say for certain, I can't be 100% sure about it but I think that is the reason. Of course the ship had been hit, but why was there such a fuss when there was no-one left on board. All that had to be done was the tow rope to be cut and her to be watched.

The other point that I would like to make now, while we're talking about the slide into war, is that around the time of the sinking of the Belgrano, three ships, the Alacrity being one of them, were carrying out their very first raids on the area around Stanley. We were told we were doing it to put the runway out of commission. I must ask the question, why were we using weaponry which exploded in the air causing maximum casualties to the Argentines? If we were there to put the runway out of commission just why were we using weapons which exploded in the air and not on the ground?

Tam Dalyell: That is a question that has been repeatedly and effectively asked by Paul Rogers and I would suggest that the panel might like to press Dr Rogers on the whole question, because you are right that it is extraordinary that those particular weapons were used if the object was to put the runway out of action. In other ways I'm very concerned now that the Argentines have the small Natra Durandel bombs that can put the £600 million international airport there out of action. What happens to our troops if there's no Phantom cover even for a matter of minutes before the sappers repair it? But that's another subject. I'm quite sure that you're right in what you say and that it's a rhetorical question, and a very damning rhetorical question.

Wade Tidbury: Do you actually think that these types of shells were used to help to make a situation around the sinking of the Belgrano?

Tam Dalyell: Yes, that's my view. And it's a dreadful thing to say.

Craig Downie: Wasn't there a suspicion of the existence of Argentine nuclear missiles which could have been used against the Task Force?

Tam Dalyell: There may have been a suspicion, but I think that they knew that they hadn't yet completed the work on the 143 tonnes of heavy water of American origin which the Argentines had bought from West Germany and that they hadn't at that time completed the nuclear cycle. Alphonsin incidentally, has either not had the will nor more likely the power to stop the development of nuclear weapons since. And just as the Israelis have nuclear weapons I'm sure that the Argentines are very close to it.

Duncan Smith: There are three questions asking why the Labour Party had not debated the Foreign Affairs Select Committee or the Franks Report.

Tam Dalyell: We did debate the Franks Report. I think I'd better give you a very candid answer, that there are those in the Party who think that to resurrect the subject simply reminds the country of Mrs Thatcher's "Finest Hour", and that it's better not to go back to it. They took the view, and correctly in a sense, that Select Committee Reports should be debated in government time. Equally there was the feeling that to go back 4 years rather than have parliamentary time on housing, the Health Service, education, unemployment and a whole number of other matters, would be misunderstood in the country. I didn't agree with that view but at least it was a view.

Thomas Thackray: Were dissenters from the general opinion of the Labour Party, such as yourself and Tony Benn who did not agree with the sending of the Task Force, silenced by senior figures of the Labour Party itself?

Tam Dalyell: No one could say that we were silenced and nor was there any pressure to be silenced. Now Michael Foot sacked me from the front bench, but on the other hand I can't hold that against him at all, because given collective responsibility, you can't have someone stridently against the view of the Shadow Cabinet and remain on the front bench. But there was never any rebuke at all. And Michael Foot, I have to tell you, behaved wholly, personally honourably, he really did.

Julia Trubridge: I come from Australia and we have tried for quite some time to instigate and to get the government to approve of a Minister for Peace. What is your opinion on this? If somebody had a position like, say minister, he would have the power of being able to report to the Prime Minister what the people think. A lot of people were dead against what was going on, but they couldn't get the message over.

Tam Dalyell: Part of the difficulty is this. In a conflict between patriotic nationalism and peace and socialism, if I can put it that way, patriotic nationalism has so often won. Look what happened to the German Labour Movement in 1914, they filed in behind the Kaiser pretty quick, and the truth is that there was in this country, a terrible amount of jingoism. Now I hope that that will never happen again because people may have been brought up a bit abruptly. If I can say to an Australian, and I spent some time up at Townsville and Cairns because of the Innisfail biological testing, with Senator George Georges and others, the Peace Movement in Australia is highly creditable. I only wish that your government, if I may say so, would be quite as outspoken as David Lange in New Zealand on the question of nuclear weapons systems.

Richard Baker: Mr Dalyell spoke of Mrs Thatcher threatening nuclear bombardment to teach them a lesson. How far is that substantiated?

Tam Dalyell: I believe it to be true that there was this conversation with naval chiefs. I have no written evidence of it.

In conclusion, if I can say it, because she might not be able to do so, one of the key events in all this was during the 1983 General Election, when that housewife of Cirencester — for such, Diana, I will describe you — cross-questioned Mrs Thatcher on the sinking of the Belgrano. At that election there was no other point in time at which the Prime Minister was so flustered, or is so well remembered by those who saw it. Had it not been also for the actions of one who is present, Clive Ponting, I doubt if it would have been possible ever to sustain a campaign to get the truth. But you see it's not just the Belgrano, because this in a sense is a pattern. Jean and Cecil Woolf thought of a title 'Patterns of Deceit', and to them I say yes it is a pattern because there are certain aspects of the bombing of Tripoli and Benghazi that fit into this. There are certain aspects of behaviour in the miners' strike and Mr David Hart's role, for a Prime Minister who said it was all a matter for the Coal Board, and certainly the whole story of the Law Officer's letter and Westlands is a story of a Prime Minister who as I said openly, inside and outside the House of Commons, has behaved as a bounder and a liar and a deceiver and a cheat and a crook. I would never ever have used such words of any other Prime Minister: certainly not of Ted Heath, certainly not of Alec Home, certainly not of Harold MacMillan, my first Prime Minister. Mrs Thatcher is responsible for bringing the good name of our country to historical ignominy.

III

Crisis Management and the Control of Risks in a Nuclear Age

Clive Ponting, Ken Coates

Clive Ponting

I'd like to start not in 1982 but in 1984 because in March of that year I was moved at very short notice to become head of the division inside the Ministry of Defence that dealt with naval operations. And the first thing that was on my desk when I got there was the letter that Tam Dalyell has already mentioned this morning from the Shadow Cabinet, questioning the Prime Minister about the accuracy of the accounts that had been given of the sinking of the Belgrano. Interestingly, I was asked by John Stanley, the Minister of State under Michael Heseltine, to prepare two answers for the Prime Minister to say: one of them would tell the truth of what had happened and the second would tell the Government's story that they had been telling for the previous two years. When these papers arrived with Michael Heseltine he decided that he was in political trouble and that I should be asked to write the full account of what took place in 1982 based on all the available documentation. This was the study that's become known as the Crown Jewels because it does contain a complete account as far as we were able to deduce it of everything that took place in April and May 1982, except interestingly for one very important omission. Although I had complete access to documents within the Ministry of Defence including the top secret intelligence reports, the one set of documents that I was refused access to were the Foreign Office telegrams from Washington and Lima over the weekend of 1st and 2nd of May. I was only allowed to see two of those telegrams which have subsequently become fairly well known, the telegrams from Washington and Lima announcing the Peruvian Peace Plan, both timed after the sinking of the Belgrano. And the Foreign Office refused to allow me access to any other telegrams — if, they said, they existed. Before I go on to try and describe what was in The Crown Jewels and the way if affects the way the war was run, I think it's important to try and understand how the Ministry of Defence works, because without that I don't think you could see any of the problems that were faced and the sort of decisions that were being taken.

The Ministry of Defence isn't a unified ministry, it's split up into three separate service departments and they are of course rivals of each other. They are not all working to exactly the same end, they are competing for money and resources most of the time, but also for prestige and position. It's the job of Ministers to attempt to set the policy between the three services. Now in 1982 John Nott was still Secretary of State but was in great disfavour with the Royal Navy because the year before he'd presided over a defence review that had virtually, in the Navy's view, seen the end of Britain's ocean going Navy. The main aircraft carrier Invincible was to be sold to the Australians, all the major landing craft with the amphibious capability were to be scrapped, the number of frigates and war ships were to be severely reduced. Now the Navy never accepted this policy, they were forced to go along with it, and all the time were attempting to get it reversed. I think the important point is that about April/May 1982 was the time at which final decisions would be taken, the ships would actually be sold or sent off to the breaker's yard. And the other important point is I think the depth of the Government's unpopularity early in 1982, when they were in an extremely difficult political situation, looking I think desperately for an issue that would restore their popularity.

Now although it's not really I suppose part of this enquiry, I think it's fascinating to actually read the Franks Committee Report on pre-April 1982, because much of what went wrong in the Conflict itself was foreshadowed then: a complete inability to actually produce a coherent policy on the Falklands. Britain was in the position of knowing, or of having decided, that they were not prepared to negotiate with the Argentines over the Falklands except on the terms set by the Falkland Islanders. That may be a reasonable position for a Government to take up if it so decides. Unfortunately they also knew and were consistently told by their intelligence sources that if they took such a decision, Argentina was quite likely to resort to military force at short notice. The neglect by the Government was to do anything about it, was actually to plan for the defence of the Islands and just to assume that something would turn up.

Well nothing did turn up and I think you have to imagine the scene in the Prime Minister's room in the House of Commons on the evening of Wednesday 30th March. The Cabinet were shell-shocked to have finally been told by their intelligence advisers that the Argentines were almost certain to invade on 2nd April. They knew there was no time to send any forces to defend the Islands and Thatcher is believed to have said that she thought their Government would fall. At this moment of crisis, uninvited, Admiral Sir Henry Leach, the Chief of the Naval Staff, walked in in full dress uniform, having arrived from a private dinner. He assured the Prime Minister that the Navy would save the Government and that if they sent a task force the Islands might be recaptured after invasion. This of course was what they wanted to hear.

At this time the Chief of the Defence Staff was not in the country, he was in New Zealand and in this sort of vacuum the Royal Navy took over the whole control of the operation. And they had to make, very early on, I think very crucial decisions about how the operation was to be controlled. Now the military from their point of view, how they see the Conflict is that they should be allowed to get on with the job without the politicians controlling them very closely. Now it's the job of the politicians of course to balance military action and diplomatic action. That's not the job of the military, the job of the military is to tell them what the forces can do and to say, "This is what we think needs to be done." But it's for the politicians to decide. Now the military were quite determined that the operation was not going to be controlled from the Ministry of Defence headquarters in Whitehall, the same building of course as Ministers were in and where ministers would have easy access to the Chiefs of Staff room and so on. They decided very early on that the operation was to be controlled by the Commander-in-Chief Fleet at Northwood, one remove from London and that all communications with Northwood would be through the Chiefs of Staff. And at the same time the actual commander of the whole Task Force would be in Northwood and there would be a commander on the spot actually running the Fleet. That was Sandy Woodward; but he never controlled any of the submarines, they were controlled separately also at Northwood.

So really you've got a very complicated picture and it turned out that during the whole of the operation the main blockage of information was not between the Falkland Islands and Northwood, but between Northwood and London. On many occasions I remember seeing John Nott's Private Secretary and he would be absolutely fuming and so would John Nott; they could not find out what was going on in the South Atlantic! They would be speaking to Northwood asking to find out where ships were, and being told, "Well it's 8,000 miles away, we've only got one satellite, we can't talk to them all, the communications are down, we don't know what's going on." Only when they motored up to Northwood would they find the complete operations picture up on the board with every ship plotted exactly where it was. And the military were not prepared to tell the politicians things that they didn't think the politicians ought to hear. They wanted to keep the operation under their own control. So the information flow was from the South Atlantic to Northwood, then Northwood to the Chiefs of Staff, and then from the Chiefs of Staff to ministers. Ministers didn't have their own knowledge of what was going on, they were dependent on other people to tell them what was happening.

And the other important factor and I think it's something perhaps for the next session, is the whole legal position because since Britain wasn't at war with Argentina there were strict limits under United Nations Charter as to what Britain could and couldn't do. It could not have open warfare and all the time the position of the forces and what they were allowed to do was strictly controlled by the Attorney General, the Government's chief legal adviser, and the Foreign Office legal advisers as well. And they set certain constraints.

Now the other way in which the operation was controlled was through these things called Rules of Engagement. These are standard, a great book of them. The Navy have them on board every ship and they are done by code, by numbers which tell them what things they may do and what things they may not do. And it's for the politicians to decide which rules to operate an engagement are actually valid at any one time. There is a whole machinery inside the Ministry of Defence for processing requests by the military for more power, and if you grant people extra rules of engagement there's more things that they can do, they can attack things in different places. Now this is the crucial thing that politicians have got to do, to balance the military's request for more power and more room to operate with the diplomatic aspect of seeking a settlement.

The other important point legally was to issue clear warnings to the Argentine as to what actions Britain would take in certain circumstances and report them to the United Nations under Article 51.

The first thing that Britain did was set up the Maritime Exclusion Zone early in April, on the 12th, the date on which the first nuclear submarine, which had been despatched from Britain before the Islands were invaded, reached the area, and could therefore start operations. After that there was another warning given on 23rd April that any approach to the Task Force would meet what was known as, 'the appropriate response.' This was designed to try and stop the Argentines shadowing the Task Force as it sailed south from Ascension Island and for the invasion of South Georgia.

Now of course all through this period Alexander Haig was shuttling between London, Washington and Argentina. The British were in a difficult position because the whole operation

couldn't have been conducted without the American support on Ascension Island. None of the ships would have had enough fuel, none of the aircraft flying off Ascension Island would have had fuel unless the Americans had provided it. There would have been no communications with the Task Force at all if by chance the Americans had not put up the communications satellite twelve months before over the South Atlantic. Also the Americans were supplying a number of sophisticated pieces of military equipment. Now in those circumstances the Government, every time Alexander Haig came to London and tried to put pressure on them to settle, knew that there was a limit to how far they could hold out against Haig. If he really put the screws on, if America was determined on a settlement, Britain might have to settle. So every time he came, the Cabinet edged a bit towards a settlement, then when he went away again the military kept asking for more room to manoeuvre and occasionally they went a little bit that way. So they were vacillating from one side to the other depending on who'd spoken to the War Cabinet last, whether it was a bit more towards diplomacy or a bit more towards military action. The crucial events that surround the sinking of the Belgrano started at the end of April with the announcement of the Total Exclusion Zone as the Task Force reached the Falkland Islands. This was actually timed to coincide with the ending of the Haig mission. The British Government already knew the proposals that Haig was going to make. They expected the Argentines to reject them and under American pressure accepted the Haig proposals, whilst expecting and hoping that the Argentines would reject. The Argentines didn't actually reject them although Haig was to take their reply as a rejection.

The crucial meeting following this took place at two o'clock in the afternoon on the 30th April in the War Cabinet. And it was at that stage knowing that the Americans had given up on the peace process and, most important, not expecting the Peruvians to suddenly pick up the whole idea again, that the Government decided it was time to move in to the military phase of the operation. Now what they decided to do without issuing any warning whatsoever was to try and sink the Argentine aircraft carrier outside the Total Exclusion Zone. Had they done so the 300 casualties on the Belgrano would have been small scale compared with the huge casualties if the aircraft carrier had indeed been sunk. They also decided, as we heard, that Port Stanley would be attacked both by sea and by air. Now there was dissent at that meeting about what was being done, as to whether what was being done was legal which perhaps fits in best in the next session, where the dissent by both the Foreign Secretary and the

Attorney General on what the Government wanted to do, was made clear.

The next day, on the Saturday, Pym was to fly to Washington to talk to the Americans. At the same time in the South Atlantic the Conqueror finally sighted the Belgrano, having been homing in for nearly 18 hours on the previous day. And it was sighted refuelling at sea with an old oil tanker. Now under the Rules of Engagement it could not be sunk outside the Exclusion Zone and Conqueror simply trailed the Belgrano as it sailed eastwards, actually towards the Task Force. Now this is I think important, because on the Saturday afternoon the Task Force was for the first time actually under attack by the Argentine airforce. At the same time Northwood knew that they had the Belgrano detected and followed and it was actually sailing towards the Task Force. Now that, as we've always been told by the Government, was supposed to be an immediate military threat. What I think is interesting is to see what the military themselves did about it, which was precisely nothing. They didn't even bother to tell the Chief of the Defence Staff in London that they had detected the Belgrano and were following it. All the time when the Task Force was actually under attack and the Belgrano was sailing towards the Task Force nothing was done, there was no attempt either by the Commander of Conqueror, Wreford-Brown, or the man in charge of the whole Task Force, Admiral Fieldhouse, to get any political decision to sink the Belgrano. They didn't even bother, as I said, to tell the Chief of the Defence Staff what had happened, so the whole of London was in ignorance as to the fact that the Belgrano had been detected and sighted. Sandy Woodward the Commander of the Task Force on the spot in the South Atlantic also knew the Belgrano had been detected and he was also the man suffering the Argentine attacks, and did nothing. He did *not* ask for permission to sink the Belgrano.

Interestingly, when Francis Pym arrived in Washington that evening, he said that there was no intention by Britain to do anything except enforce the Exclusion Zone. Yet at the same time, the day before, he had been present at a War Cabinet meeting that had authorised the sinking of the aircraft carrier *outside* of the Exclusion Zone. And for all he knew — and indeed he had actually signed a Minute of Dissent to the Prime Minister about the way in which it was being done — when he arrived in Washington the aircraft carrier could actually have been sunk. Yet he was still trying to claim that Britain was only enforcing the Exclusion Zone and was taking no military action outside of the Zone at all: all part of the Government's general attempt to paint the picture that Britain was only reacting to Argentine attacks rather than stepping up the military campaign itself.

Now the crucial day for the sinking of the Belgrano is the Sunday the 2nd of May. What happened was, early in the morning, about eight o'clock in the morning London Time, Woodward, the man on the spot in the South Atlantic, suddenly ordered the Conqueror to sink the Belgrano outside the Exclusion Zone. He was immediately told by Northwood that he had no authority to do so and the order was rescinded — but the Chiefs of Staff were meeting at the same time in London. They believed that the Belgrano was still sailing towards the Task Force. In fact it wasn't, but they didn't know that at the time. What they asked for then was not authority to sink the Belgrano but authority to sink any Argentine warship anywhere. Admiral Lewin, the Chief of the Defence Staff, left London to go to Northwood to talk to Fieldhouse before he went to Chequers to meet the War Cabinet. When he got to Northwood it is believed for the first time he was aware that the Belgrano was actually sailing towards the Task Force. He had not been told for nearly 24 hours and had decided to ask for authority to sink all Argentine warships without knowing this. There was the debate at Northwood (Tam says he knows what went on, but we could find no official record of what was said), and then Lewin went to Chequers to talk to the Prime Minister and the rest of the War Cabinet. And, in what is admitted by all politicians present at the time to have been a meeting that lasted no more than 15 minutes on the doorstep of Chequers, he obtained authority from the War Cabinet to attack all Argentine warships anywhere on the high seas. Now this is absolutely crucial, it seems to me, when we are talking about political control of the military. In that quarter of an hour, what sort of questions did the War Cabinet actually ask Lewin? What reaction did they have as to what the Argentines might do next? What did they think about the escalation that they were taking? The day before, the Prime Minister received a Minute from the Foreign Secretary and the Attorney-General suggesting that any action along those lines without an adequate public warning to Argentina might well be illegal. No public warning was to be issued about the decision to sink any ship anywhere on the high seas. Ministers have said since that they didn't know at the time which way the Belgrano was sailing. Maybe they should have asked. What sort of decisions were they really taking, not even knowing where the ship was, which way it was going and what the threat was to the Task Force. Was it really sufficient for the Chief of the Defence Staff to come along and say, "I'd like to sink all the Argentine ships anywhere," and for it immediately to be granted within a very short discussion with no formal papers in front of them whatsoever?

Anyway, in that quarter of an hour the decision was taken and at 1.30 in the afternoon Northwood signalled the whole of the Task Force that they could now sink Argentine ships anywhere on the high seas. What is now interesting is what happens on board H.M.S. Conqueror in the South Atlantic, because when that signal was received a very strange thing happened, and it is very difficult to piece together exactly what Commander Wreford-Brown was doing. Because in March 1984 when we looked through the log of Conqueror, not the one that has subsequently gone missing, he wrote in the book that he had not understood the order when it was given. What he did do was immediately signal Northwood that the Belgrano had turned away from the Task Force some six to seven hours before and was now consistently sailing back towards the Argentine mainland. I would suggest that that is probably the nearest an officer in the Royal Navy would actually get to saying, "Do you really want me to sink this ship?" And he waited; *twice* in the period after that he again received the disturbing signal that he could now sink the Belgrano, and he didn't do so. The log book says that the orders were garbled.

Now what happens in Northwood when for the first time they find out that the Belgrano is not actually sailing towards the Task Force but away from it and has been for the last six or seven hours? The answer is, absolutely nothing. They get the signal, simply copy it to London, to the military end of London, and nothing else happens. Ministers were never told at that stage that the Belgrano had turned around. The military didn't tell them because of course the military had obtained the one decision that they wanted from the politicians, which was authority to sink Argentine warships wherever they were. Of course they would argue that it was now irrelevant which way the Belgrano was sailing because the decision by ministers allowed them to sink it whatever it was doing. In the end Conqueror went in and sank the Belgrano.

The next day, even on the admissions by ministers, they knew of the Peruvian Peace Plan. They did not at that stage make any attempt to call off the further attack by H.M.S. Conqueror on the surviving warships that had been escorting the Belgrano and indeed the Conqueror went back in an attempt to sink the two escorting destroyers, which of course it was entirely able to do under the Rules of Engagement agreed by ministers. The attack was actually called off on 4th May not by ministers but by Commander-in-Chief Fleet, Admiral Fieldhouse, who said he was not going to have British warships sinking Argentine ships that might be rescuing survivors from the Belgrano. And it was not until three days after that that Britain actually issued a warning to the Argentine saying that they would sink any Argentine ship outside of Argentine territorial waters. In other words five days after they had decided to do so they finally told the U.N. and the Argentines what their new policy was.

Now I think that sort of saga has absolutely terrible consequences and implications for a real crisis. This is a bad enough crisis as it was, an action taken by the British that escalated the conflict enormously and led on obviously to the sinking of the Sheffield, taken in circumstances where it is far from clear that ministers ever began to consider what the consequences of escalating the conflict were. If that sort of action is being taken in a major and fundamental crisis say in Europe, when Britain might be involved with NATO in either an attack, or a threatened attack, by the Soviet Union, where nuclear weapons might well be used, it has absolutely profound implications for the idea of political control. Because all the theory that's written about how you control nuclear warfare assumes that politicians are people who sit there rationally and coolly deciding the best possible course, having in front of them every available scrap of information that's been carefully passed on to them by the military. It is all very different than that. Politicians are sitting there full of prejudices and their own fears, surrounded by bits of information that have been passed on, some of it up-to-date, some of it out-of-date, and all of it can lead to enormous misjudgements and consequences when people are not prepared to consider the possible implications of what they're doing. It was all summed up I think by a Permanent Secretary in Whitehall who was very close to all the deliberations of the War Cabinet, when he said in May 1982, "Well if ministers behave like this when they're in the big league with the Russians I'm off to the desert island."

Ken Coates

Mr Chairman, members of the enquiry, my contribution will be a short one but I have brought with me a copy of an exchange of letters with Mr Perez de Cuellar the Secretary-General of the United Nations. I want to explore some of the questions which arise from the exchange.

In 1983 when various people present in this audience were actually involved in trying to discover the truth about these events, there was a general election and in the course of that it seemed to me important to seek international opinion on the implications of the information that was coming to light over here. So I asked the Secretary-General two questions. The first one covers ground which has already been discussed this morning and this afternoon. It concerns the legality of the actions which have just been described. The query which seemed to me to require attention was not simply that which apparently engaged the appropriate officers of the Government who were worried about conformity with the United Nations Charter. I thought then and I think today that there is another important international instrument which needed to be considered. And that is the document known as the Nuremburg Principles which was unanimously ratified by the United Nations immediately after the Nuremburg Trials of Nazi war criminals after the Second World War. That document attempted to establish legal boundaries as to what was and what was not permissible military action. And it defined in its Principle Number 6 a crime of violence against the peace, if I can cite this infraction, 'It is a war crime against peace to plan, prepare, initiate or wage a war in violation of international agreement or assurances.' And the question that I requested some advice from the Secretary-General on was whether the decision in the United nations to approve Resolution 502 was in fact an agreement the breach of which might be taken as a violation of Principle Number 6.

Now naturally the Secretary-General replied in the way he is bound to reply. He said this was an interesting question but that it could not be answered unless it was asked by a member state. And that's the first question I wanted to table on your agenda Mr Chairman, because although the Secretary-General governs an organisation which is ruled by strict protocol, there is nonetheless a reality to the problem and citizens of a democratic society have not only a right to form an opinion about that but I would suggest they also may well have a duty to form such an opinion when the evidence which is gathered becomes so overwhelming. But that is only the first of the queries, the second is a little more difficult to explain.

The second of my queries concerned the possibility that nuclear weapons had been taken into the South Atlantic area. And that question is difficult for two different distinct sets of reasons. First of all it's difficult in law and secondly it is extremely difficult to establish with any security the factual circumstances. Were or were not nuclear weapons taken into the area and if they were, was that fact a breach of international law or not? The law in question happens to be one which is of enormous importance to the future of arms control and disarmament in the world. Because the law in question is that established by the treaty called the Treaty of Tlatelolco, which is a suburb of Mexico City, which is the first international agreement making a densely populated area into a Nuclear Free Zone. There are other Zones, in Antarctica, on the sea bed, from which nuclear weapons are excluded by international agreement. But the decision that the whole of South

America would exclude nuclear weapons was a major breakthrough for a principle which had been canvassed over many years by statesmen and scholars from a wide number of countries. And that breakthrough, for such it was, was celebrated a couple of years ago with the award of the Nobel Peace Prize to the Mexican Ambassador in charge of the negotiations on the Treaty and to the distinguished Swedish peace researcher who was one of the proponents of Nuclear Free Zones. So the question at issue is, did the terms of the Treaty of Tlatelolco apply in this case and in what way? And secondly, was the conduct of the British Government, or was it not, a breach of those terms?

And the evidence that I want to have exploration of is by no means as clear as the evidence which you've been hearing up to now. And I do not at all propose that the enquiry could on the basis of such information as has yet been uncovered, be able to pronounce a firm verdict as it were. And I do believe that it is extremely important to keep this file open and to invite further evidence from whosoever may possess it. Because the truth of the matter is that if the Treaty of Tlatelolco is breached, if it has been breached, this is a major problem for the central United Nations strategy for arms control and disarmament. You will find that one of the main commitments, the very basic commitments of the 1978 Resolution of the United Nations Special Assembly on Disarmament governs this question of Nuclear Free Zones which frankly the majority of the delegates present thought to be the only acceptable and democratically approachable road to non-proliferation of nuclear weapons. There are many criticisms of the Non-Proliferation Treaty which to many people seems to be a conspiracy by nuclear powers to police the non-nuclear world. But Nuclear Free Zones have the same effect of non-proliferation by an act of popular volition, by choice by peoples and statesmen within an area which defines itself. Now I don't wish to abuse your hospitality Mr Chairman by saying more about Nuclear Free Zones except to stress that this is a central problem for the future not only of this country but of the world, that if we allow a Nuclear Free Zone to be violated then we do jeopardise far more than the secure future of the two contenders in this conflict.

Now let us then briefly look at what would happen under the Treaty if it were to be violated. And the argument there is quite complex but I think I can simplify it by explaining that countries outside Latin America can endorse the Treaty under one or both of two additional protocols. And these two protocols apply in a nutshell to colonial powers holding territories in South America but resident outside the continent, in the first case, and to nuclear powers in the second case. So the British Governments falls into both categories. Now the Argentine Government did make a complaint that the British Government had violated the Treaty by sending the Conqueror, which is a nuclear-powered submarine, into the area and by sinking the Belgrano through its agency. And that complaint has been widely discussed and normally dismissed because the terms of the Treaty can be argued to exempt weapons which are propelled by nuclear fuels from the category of weapons which are banned from the Zone under the Treaty. The Treaty is defined in such a way as to give the impression that it only excludes uncontrolled nuclear explosions and nuclear propulsions are legitimate. Lawyers will argue about that for quite some time because it is arguable that the use of nuclear propulsion in a submarine which is bent upon destruction could be included within the range of prohibitions that the Treaty establishes. And that's a technical question which seems to me to be worth professional attention.

But of course the real question is not whether or not nuclear submarines entered the area. The real question is whether nuclear weapons entered the area. And before we can determine that we have to see that there are two areas which could be covered under the Treaty. If Britain interprets its signature to the Tlatelolco protocol as being the signature of a colonial power it could argue that only the territorial waters then existing in the immediate area of the Falkland Islands were prohibited to nuclear weapons. If Britain interprets its signature to Protocol Two of the Treaty as a nuclear power as being the governing protocol then the area in question is enormously wider because the Treaty defines a vast area of the South Atlantic as falling into the territory which is guaranteed by its terms. In fact they simply divide the Atlantic Ocean down the middle and not only the Falkland Islands but a wide measure of many hundreds of square miles of sea to the east of the Falkland Islands would fall securely within the prohibited area into which nuclear weapons must not be brought. So that is the problem we are facing. Then we have the difficulty about the evidence. And it may be that some of those who are in a much better position than I am to know what was happening and whose enquiries are further advanced, can answer some of these questions far more satisfactorily than I can.

There are reports to the effect that the British fleet steamed southwards in a vast hurry in a manner which made it impossible for it to divest itself of nuclear weapons before it arrived in the South Atlantic. As far as I can see these reports begin in The Times in late 1982 and are then picked up and repeated and confirmed by other sources. They are reported in a study by the Stockholm International Peace Research Institute where these issues are discussed in a very balanced manner. Tam Dalyell seized on these reports and conducted one of his persistent enquiries along this dimension and to the best of my knowledge no satisfactory answers have been given to the questions which he raised. Tam of course was not merely dependent upon the media for his sources of information and maybe he can divulge some more about this matter which is not yet on the record. What is specifically said and was stated by Tam Dalyell in his first book on this question is that the ship H.M.S. Sheffield was sunk whilst carrying a large arsenal of nuclear depth charges, which he claimed were standard issue for ships of that class. Subsequently this argument has become more complex and has provoked some denials from people who may not be qualified to issue denials. In a nutshell the Swedish Merchant Fleet provided two ships under the general family name of Stenor, which went to the South Atlantic and which after the war were retained to salvage something from H.M.S. Sheffield. And it was reported in the pacifist press in Sweden that they were salvaging these nuclear weapons. The New Statesman, a Duncan Campbell enquiry, investigated these stories and reported that they were not founded. Duncan Campbell believed that the Stenor ships were searching for code books which had been sunk when the ship went down. I can't throw any light on this question. It does seem perhaps to be a little strange to go to such enormous lengths to retrieve code books however important they may be, because most people might think that they would be secure in the place to which they had been consigned. I only raise the question because I think it is so important that it should be adequately answered, that it seems to me we should go on asking it until it is.

Now of course there have been a number of denials. The British Government was quizzed by the enforcement body which polices the Tlatelolco Treaty, to which complaints were made not only by the Argentine Government but also by Panama. And denials were made but the denials were blanket denials which fall uneasily between the areas I've just defined. First of all the Government always insisted that it never answered questions about whether its ships were nuclear-armed or not, and that has been repeated at various intervals. Secondly, specifically, it has been said that the Government never breached its obligations under the Treaty of Tlatelolco but there remains a vast ambiguity because the Government did not, in saying this, specify which protocol it was obeying, whether that which would respect a three mile territorial limit around the Falkland Islands or whether that which would be much wider. I apologise for the length of that intervention Mr Chairman. I hope very much that some of these questions might receive firmer answers as a result of your enquiries this weekend. I do believe this is a matter of burning importance because I do not think that mankind is likely to survive to the end of this century if we torpedo, with the Belgrano, the most hopeful armament control measure that has yet been invented by mankind.

John Ferguson: Thank you. There are one or two questions which I'd like — I think they can be answered very briefly — to put to Clive Ponting. First Tam Dalyell gave the view this morning that the sinking of the Belgrano was essentially a political decision. In the way you started you were suggesting that it was essentially a military decision. Is there a conflict?

Clive Ponting: No I don't think so. I mean obviously the military wanted it, the military had for days if not weeks been suggesting that the way to clear the thing up was simply to let them go and get on with it, and do whatever they thought had to be done. The final decision to do it at that particular time was certainly a political decision, one that was taken if not by the whole of the War Cabinet at least by the Prime Minister, whichever other members of the War Cabinet happened to be at Chequers before the meeting started.

John Ferguson: Then do you think that the original refusal to sink the Belgrano which you referred to, was because the Belgrano was outside the Exclusion Zone?

Clive Ponting: It's almost impossible to say why the military on the day before the Belgrano was actually sunk, decided that it wasn't a threat; it wasn't something that they had to ask the politicians to do something about, because at that stage they didn't have the authority to sink it outside the Exclusion Zone. Yet all the time the politicians have said that the one reason it had to be sunk was because it was a direct threat to the Task Force. Now the only time at which it was a direct threat was on the day before it was sunk when it was sailing towards the Task Force rather than away from it, and at that stage the military didn't ask for anything to be done even though the Task Force was under attack. Now presumably they didn't think it was much of a threat.

John Ferguson: Third, you indicated that Woodward gave orders to sink the Belgrano at 8 a.m. on Sunday morning, Northwood said no and this was rescinded. This is not in the Foreign Affairs Committee evidence as I remember. Is the evidence for this documentation you used at the ministry?

Clive Ponting: Yes, it is public knowledge now that that took place.

John Ferguson: Thank you. Can we get the timing straight because I think this is very important. You've indicated that at 8 a.m. London Time, then at 9 a.m. London Time, according to the report the Belgrano reversed direction.

Clive Ponting: Yes, correct.

John Ferguson: That was informed to London and do we know at what time?

Clive Ponting: 3 o'clock in the afternoon.

John Ferguson: 3 o'clock in the afternoon, and the actual sinking?

Clive Ponting: 8 o'clock in the evening.

Richard Baker: Just two points...could you explain a bit more about the chain of command? Was the entire Falkland Operation including the Army and the Royal Airforce under command of the Naval Commander-in-Chief?

Clive Ponting: Yes. Because the Navy started the operation off before the Chiefs of Staff could get control of it. It was decided that Fieldhouse, that's the Command-in-Chief Fleet, would be in command of the whole operation. He had both a military and an airforce deputy as well, that was later in April. Indeed that certainly raised great problems later in May after the invasion where most of the important decisions were actually Army or Airforce decisions.

Richard Baker: The other point was, I didn't quite get this point about the Swedish report and it seems terribly important that either that can be substantiated or rejected... Who exactly in Sweden reported what they'd found? Had they found a nuclear weapon or evidence of it? Have they published this claim? Who exactly are they?

Ken Coates: The pacifist press in Sweden reported that the Stenor ships had been commissioned to fish for nuclear weapons. That report was denied in the New Statesman by Duncan Campbell in a report which appeared during 1984, on the grounds that the ships were not carrying nuclear weapons and that intelligence sources had informed Mr Campbell that the fishing did take place but was for code books. The pacifist press in Sweden may be very well in error on this question. What is at issue it seems to me is what is the source that Mr Campbell, who is here in this country, can throw light on. It doesn't on the surface seem to be adequate. There's no question but that the Stenor ships did stay in the South Atlantic and one of them was actually taken over by the Royal Navy, and that the Stenor ships were fishing for something. The question I put to the enquiry is, can we find out what they were fishing for? Can we invite the public, especially those persons with direct involvement to tell us what they were fishing for?

Richard Baker: But then even if the Swedish pacifist press was correct, the most that can be said was that they were looking. No one has actually reported that they found any evidence of nuclear weapons. They reported, if I understand you correctly, that they were looking for them and the result was not reported by the Swedish pacifist press or anybody else.

Ken Coates: No, as far as I know there has been no claim that the Stenor ships actually landed nuclear weapons. But if they were looking for them it would presume that somebody thought they were there.

Clive Ponting: Can I just add one thing to that and that is another article by Duncan Campbell in either November or December last year which dealt with the whole question of how many nuclear weapons Britain had, in which he alleged that what had taken place during the Falklands was that ministers, in the middle of April, suddenly found out that three quarters of Britain's Naval nuclear weapons were in Ascension Island, on board the Task Force; and that they had not known this beforehand and indeed they had not known that naval ships sailed with nuclear weapons on board in peace time; that there was a fearful row in the War Cabinet between the political and the military which resulted in the Task Force staying at Ascension Island for three days whilst all the nuclear weapons were offloaded, because the politicians were not prepared to lose what few British nuclear weapons at sea there were if one of the ships had gone down. That's what he reported.

Wade Tidbury: A point about the Stenor ships from Sweden, are we talking about the Seaspread? Because if we are, that ship I can confirm was shortly after the surrender detailed to go to the exact position of the sinking of the Sheffield. Now if that ship was going to rescue documents, which is very unlikely, then it should have been detailed many, many weeks before when the Sheffield was recently sunk. Every ship in the force would have carried a weighted bag which was to be thrown in an emergency. The bag would then have been thrown overboard should the ship have been sinking straight away. The Sheffield didn't sink straight away, it was several days before it sank. I would like to suggest that the losing of the nuclear weapons on the Sheffield was something which would have been considered dangerous, that's why great urgency was placed in towing the Sheffield away from the Falklands by H.M.S. Ghana for several days till the Sheffield actually sunk when the sea came up and water got into the hold.

Ken Coates: It is precisely this kind of evidence which I think this enquiry can do an enormous service by stimulating people to testify. The point I am making is simply that the Treaty of Tlatelolco must be rendered enforceable. It is a piece of patrimony of peace movements and enlightened people of the world and that is why I think that even such sketchy evidence as I was able to find needs further investigation because this kind of story is uncomfortable and requires attention.

Unknown contributor: I'd just like to mention that... in February 1983 I was told by a correspondent that his brother who was supplying on one of the ships, actually loaded nuclear devices on to his ship before they actually sailed for the Falklands and he was talking about a conversation he'd had with his brother. He said that at that point...

Thacher Alexander: Could you please comment on the composition of the so-called War Cabinet, particularly the inclusion of the chairman of the Conservative Party?

Clive Ponting: Obviously the Whitehall doctrine is that the Prime Minister can chose who she likes to be on the War Cabinet. Having said that, obviously there are certain people who have to be there, like Pym as Foreign Secretary, Nott as Defence Secretary and so on. After that it's very much up to choice. Whitelaw was there as somebody whose judgement she trusts. Now the interesting thing is I think the line up there: something like Pym certainly against military action most of the time, trying to seek a diplomatic solution; Nott interestingly tending that way very often and often Whitelaw as well. I think Parkinson was put there not only to handle the public relations side of it but also as a strong supporter of the Prime Minister to back her up in Cabinet if it got rough, you know if the three senior other ministers started trying to take a different line.

Thacher Alexander: I've got a supplementary I'd like to ask. One, since his trial does he believe that he is watched by persons unknown and secondly, is it likely that even here and now there are representatives from either the Ministry of Defence or....?

Clive Ponting: I honestly don't know, I wouldn't know. You never know do you?

Thomas Thackray: It's a more general question which expands on the Belgrano case itself. I would like to ask Clive Ponting to comment on the difficult role the Civil Service is being forced into by ministers' actions. These actions can be seen as questionable at least in the Westland leak and immoral in the case of the sinking of the Belgrano. Are civil servants accountable to Parliament despite their increasingly political role and I refer especially to the silencing of the civil servants in the Westlands Affair?

Clive Ponting: That's an enormously wide question. I think the problem with this is that there are no rules in this country set down as to how ministers are supposed to be accountable to Parliament or exactly what the Civil Service is supposed to do or not to do. I would take the position that most of the time the Government wouldn't actually work unless civil servants are loyal to whichever Government it is of the day. And it's for the electorate to throw out the Government when they get tired of it. But, and I think a big but, is what happens when the Government starts doing something that's either unconstitutional or deliberately suppressing information, lying or whatever. Because the civil servant is going to be the one person who's in a position to actually know what is going on and if ministers aren't prepared to say, there's no way under the current system that Parliament or anybody else is going to find out. The whole of the British system is run simply on conventions, the convention that ministers will answer questions truthfully in the House of Commons when they're asked. If they decide to start lying, there are virtually no sanctions against them except for a civil servant to say what's going on. I don't think you can stand for the position of saying that a civil servant has to be totally loyal to the Government whatever it does. If it steps over a line, in the end it's going to be the civil servant who has to be accountable either to Parliament or the public interest in some way or other and who's got to say what's going on. Because nobody else is going to be able to.

Thomas Thackray: How can civil servants counter this when they find themselves in this position? I mean they can resign but is there any other means by which they can make themselves...

Clive Ponting: Under the current system resigning wouldn't make any difference. It wouldn't have made the slightest difference if I had resigned first and then spilt the beans about what was going on. I would still have been prosecuted. It's still an offence under Section 2, or a likely offence under Section 2, to say what you know about what's been going on in Government after you've resigned, it doesn't absolve you from Section 2 as it stands at the moment.

Thomas Thackray: What about the Civil Servants' Union?

Clive Ponting: Well I mean the Union of the top civil servants, the First Division Association, has actually tried to draft a code of ethics that says what civil servants should do and what they shouldn't do. I think there should be some sort of outside body, whether the Ombudsman or something, a Committee of Privy Councillors or somebody, that a civil servant can go to and say look this is what is going on and this is what ministers have decided to do, and I don't think this is right. And you've also got to have some sort of system that protects the civil servant's job and position after he's done that. And that is in fact the system they've got in America, where under an American Act civil servants are required and asked to do this sort of thing.

Joan Hyams (World Disarmament Campaign): What I'd like to ask you is whether crews of ships have to know whether they are carrying nuclear weapons and whether those who load those nuclear weapons are naval staff or whether they are dockers? And that's of particular importance because the T.G.W.U. and the N.U.S. as they might be involved, both of those unions are supporting the World Disarmament Campaign policy of trying to get the implementation of the 1978 United Nations Declaration on World Disarmament.

Clive Ponting: The problem is that some ships carry nuclear weapons in peace time, some do not. The problem for any member of the crew is that they also carry dummy nuclear weapons as well, that to all intents and purposes look exactly the same and are designed to be drill rounds on which they practice. So I would suspect that most of the people don't actually know whether it's a live nuclear weapon or a dummy nuclear weapon, they all look the same. I wonder whether the dockers who load them would know the difference either because one is designed to look exactly like the other.

Wade Tidbury: I'd like to ask Clive Ponting about statements in Parliament after the sinking of the Belgrano regarding the actual threat to the fleet of the Belgrano. Was it known amongst the people you were working with that contrary to what was said in Parliament the weapons on the Belgrano were not Exocets? The Belgrano did not carry Exocets. Did you actually know at the time that it was sailing away from the fleet? And was it known that the escort ships were carrying Exocets?

Clive Ponting: I think it's difficult to know exactly what was known at the time. At some point somebody seems to have made the mistake of saying that the Belgrano carried Exocets, which it certainly did not and as you say it was the destroyers that did and therefore should have been considered as much more of a threat than a 1930s ageing cruiser. I think what is quite interesting is, if you look, I mean Tam Dalyell has said that he has got a copy of the original text of John Nott's statement for 4th May, which would have been written by the Civil Service, which did not say that the Belgrano was detected on the 2nd May, it did not make that mistake. It said that the Belgrano was attacked at 8 o'clock on 2nd May, which is correct. And that it was Nott himself who altered it to 'detected' at 8 p.m. on 2nd May, which he knew at the time when he said it, that it was not true because he had been present at Chequers when he'd been told that Conqueror already had Belgrano trailed earlier on 2nd May. So it shows that the Civil Service actually knew what the truth was or some aspects of it as early as 4th May and it was ministers who were deliberately changing the answers.

Wade Tidbury: There's one point I'd like to come back to, transmitted on the World Service broadcast of the debate in

Parliament: ministers said that the Belgrano was carrying Exocets. "Jane's Fighting Ships" which every ship carries showed that this was in fact false....

Clive Ponting: What made them say that I just don't know. I mean they ought to have been briefed quite clearly that the Belgrano didn't have Exocets, nobody else made that mistake, apart from ministers.

Bill Hawthorne: I'd like to ask Clive Ponting whether in his view the conduct of the Falklands War supports the view that in another crisis of sufficient gravity the decision to use the British nuclear deterrent could be taken by the military rather than by the politicians?

Clive Ponting: I'm not sure it shows that. I think what it shows is that in any sort of crisis like that politicians are going to be under pressure from the military to take military solutions and it's for the politicians to step back from that and think about other things. To be fair I don't think you can expect the military to take that sort of judgement. They will say as they did say during the Falklands, "We must do this in order to defend our ships or whatever." You would expect them to say that. It's for ministers to take the much more difficult judgement about balancing diplomacy and other things. The exact way in which British nuclear weapons would be launched is based on the assumption that only the Prime Minister can order those weapons to be fired.

Richard Baker: Does that apply to tactical nuclear weapons used by the Army?

Clive Ponting: Tactical nuclear weapons used by the Army do not have British nuclear warheads on them. They are British delivery systems with American warheads on them under dual key, so that both the British and the Americans have to release the warhead beforehand. So there has to be political authority to release on both sides.

Alan Brownjohn: I should like to ask about crisis management with regard to the role of Francis Pym....

Clive Ponting: I would have thought that what the evidence shows is that the British Government thought by the end of April that the peace process was finished, that the Haig shuttle had collapsed and that was the end of it and that they were now fairly free to get on with the military side of the war. And that Pym was being sent to America not to discuss peace but to discuss American assistance during the next stage of the war. The Haig shuttle having collapsed it was now a case of discussing with the Americans what assistance they were going to give us in the mounting of the operation from Ascension Island and elsewhere, and obviously diplomatic support as well. I think what happened was that when

Pym got to Washington he found the situation was rather different and that suddenly the Peruvians had started up the process again. Now what happened the night of the 1st May is a subject of immense dispute. Haig says he saw Pym and indeed negotiated with him that evening. Pym says he never saw Haig and never left the British Embassy until the Sunday morning Washington Time which is about midday lunchtime London. And only at that stage, he claims, did he even begin to become aware of the Peruvian proposals i.e. at about the time that the Cabinet was already deciding to sink the Belgrano. Now that is what he says. Haig does not say that. He says he was negotiating all night with the Peruvians and indeed with Pym as well and that their discussion was then down to a matter of words over the plan, individual words. Whereas Pym says no, it was all in terms of vague generalities and nothing concrete had been said.

Alan Brownjohn: May I have a follow up to that question? What reason do you think there was for allowing you access to only one set of Foreign Office telegrams?

Clive Ponting: Well, you've got to draw your own conclusions I think. The only telegrams I was allowed to see, or indeed they said 'others if they exist I was not allowed to see', were the two that are already public, which are the 10.15 telegram from Washington and the one about an hour later from Lima which give the first details of the plans which the Peruvians were negotiating. Now interestingly the Government has slightly changed — here you have to be a student of Whitehall nuances of wording — their explanation. Thatcher's letter to the Shadow Cabinet of April 1984 says the first indications of the Peruvian Peace Plan were not known in London until three hours after the sinking, which is the Washington telegram. What they now say is, the first *authoritative* indications were not available. That, in Whitehall terms, is an admission that there were unauthoritative indications earlier. Now it may well be that what they are trying to say is, that the first time we actually knew all seven points of the Peruvian Peace Plan written down on one piece of paper formally was at 10.15. That is not incompatible with knowing bits of what was going on a long time before.

Mark Birtles: Would a change in the Government necessarily lead to disclosure of all the facts and could this disclosure be hampered by the 30 Year Rule, or have unminuted decisions been taken which would require admissions by the decision makers?

Clive Ponting: There are two points here really. First as I suspect in a lot of cases of modern government, an awful lot of the stuff doesn't actually get written down on pieces of paper, telephone calls and all the rest of it. Even under the 30 Year Rule you cannot necessarily expect to get all the pieces of paper. The Government still has the right to withold documents longer than 30 years if they want to. It will be interesting to see in January how much of the Suez papers, which become available on January 1st, are actually still there. There are very strong stories that the most incriminating documents on Suez which actually show the deliberate deception, have been shredded and got rid of. But any government, a new government could order a formal enquiry into the sinking. This is one of the problems with the way British government works, because the Government controls a majority in Parliament it can stop Parliament setting up an enquiry. But a new government with a majority in the House could get a vote through to set up a formal Tribunal of Inquiry, and in the 1921 Tribunal of Inquiries Act this would actually require everybody to answer questions on oath as to what took place in 1982, if they wanted to do it. Although that of course is a purely political decision.

IV

Was it Illegal to Sink the Belgrano?

Diana Gould, Clive Ponting, Eric Ogden

Diana Gould

In November 1985 the Government published a White Paper giving its observations on the findings of the Foreign Affairs Committee Report which was published in July 1985. There was never a Parliamentary debate. In the White Paper the Government very carefully omits any part of the Majority Report which is critical of its conduct. For example in paragraph 19 of the White Paper it accepts the Majority decision that Sir John Nott's statements were made to the House in good faith, but omits the rest of the paragraph 9.10 of the Report which queries the 'perpetuation of the substance of Sir John Nott's statement so long after the event.' The White Paper admits that Ministers knew the precise course of the Belgrano in November 1982, but does not refer to the Majority Report's statement in paragraph 9.17, 'Nevertheless, we cannot fully understand why, when Ministers were informed in November 1982 of the Belgrano's change of course on 2nd May 1982, this information was not more quickly revealed to the House and the error in Sir John Nott's statement on this point put right.'

Were the true facts kept from Parliament and therefore from the world to hide the fact that the Belgrano was not an immediate threat and that the sinking was therefore contrary to International Law?

Article 2 of the United Nations calls upon all members to settle their international disputes by peaceful means.

Article 51 which allows the inherent right of self-defence if an armed attack occurs is the one exception to the general rule and hence it has always been understood that it must be interpreted very carefully. Acts of self-defence must take place directly, that is in response to an immediate threat, otherwise the use of force becomes retaliation. They must be proportional to the original act and according to most experts cannot be pre-emptive since armed aggression has to precede acts of self-defence. Pre-emption being the act of attacking first to forestall hostile action, this precludes taking action against a potential threat — a threat to the mission! — under Article 51.

Otherwise, the invoking of pre-emptive self-defence could be an excuse for unimaginable acts of armed agression. The United Kingdom is on record, on a previous occasion at the United Nations, of categorically rejecting pre-emptive self-defence; its representative then stating that armed military operations carried out under that pretext did not fall within the concept of self-defence in International Law. That is Reference A/36/PV. 53 in the United Nations Security Council.

A definition of the act of self-defence, given by a former U.S. Secretary of State is that it must be an instant response, leaving no choice of means and no moment for deliberatioin.

Unless there is a declaration of war, International waters remain open to ships of all nations and the Royal Navy has in the past played an important role in maintaining this right. War was *not* declared and during the weekend of the 1st and 2nd May 1982 a peaceful solution was being actively sought by the Peruvians and also by the United Nations Secretary-General, Perez de Cuellar. Admiral of the Fleet, Lord Lewin is on record as saying in evidence to the Foreign Affairs Committee, 'you see there was not a war.' Those are his own words in the Report.

The action taken by the War Cabinet in establishing Exclusion Zones appears to contradict the later interpretation of Article 51. In his evidence again, Lord Lewin agrees with M.P. Nigel Spearing that the 200 mile radius chosen for the Total Exclusion Zone was based on the distance certain nations claim for territorial waters. This choice of area would appear to be all we could legally claim. The Total Exclusion Zone took effect on 30th April and at this stage we did not appear to think we could deny Argentina International waters.

Were we not also attempting to safeguard the passage of the Task Force by emphasizing the difference between rights of passage in International as opposed to territorial waters?

The Government White Paper of November 1985 states that the establishment of a Maritime Exclusion Zone and the Total Exclusion Zone did not preclude action in self-defence outside the zone and bases the legality of the sinking of the Belgrano on the warning of 23rd April 1982 which stated that the approach of any warship that could amount to a threat to interfere with the *mission* of the British forces in the South Atlantic would encounter the *appropriate* response.

According to the 'Clarification Statement' of 7th May 1982, five days after the sinking of the Belgrano, Britain warned that we would regard any Argentine warships more than 12 miles from the mainland coast of South America as hostile and deal with them accordingly. Was it reasonable to assume that prior to this statement Argentina knew that we were effectively denying them International waters without declaring a state of war?

If our subsequent interpretation of the warning of 23rd April is correct, what was the charade that took place on the 30th April?

Before a change of Rules of Engagement the Mandarins Committee, chaired by the Cabinet Secretary and consisting of the permanent under-secretaries of the ministers of the War Cabinet, met in order to brief the ministers. Such a meeting occurred before the change of Rules of Engagement on the 30th April which allowed our forces to attack the Argentine aircraft carrier 25 de Mayo and which hinged on the range of the carrier's weapons, that is its aircraft. It excluded the carrier's escorts because in the words again of Admiral Lewin to the Foreign Affairs Committee they were, 'only armed with Exocet and would not be a threat until they came within about 40 miles.'

There was no further meeting of the Mandarin's Committee before the change of Rules of Engagement on 2nd May which allowed the sinking of any Argentine warship no matter what its weapons' range was, and hence the Belgrano, with a maximum gun range of 13 miles was attacked.

It is alleged that Francis Pym, the Foreign Secretary, was not happy about the change of Rules of Engagement made on 30th April to allow the sinking of the carrier. Admiral Lewin told the Foreign Affairs Committee, 'I know Mr Pym and the Attorney General wrote a letter to the Prime Minister afterwards, and I think their concern was that if the submarine did find itself in a position to attack the aircraft carrier 25 de Mayo, in public perception and the international opinion perception, this might be going further than Article 51.' An unofficial version of the letter Mr Pym is said to have sent to the Prime Minister on 1st May, before departing for the United States, is actually printed in the Foreign Affairs Committee Report. It appears to form the basis for the Clarification Statement that was eventually sent on 7th May, five days after the Belgrano was sunk.

So, here we have the Foreign Secretary, obviously worried about the escalation of hostilities that sinking an aircraft carrier would imply, journeying to Washington to confer with Alexander Haig, the U.S. Secretary of State, who had been engaged in shuttle diplomacy to attempt to find a peaceful settlement. What would be the Foreign Secretary's reaction when he received a telephone call informing him of a further change of Rules of Engagement which allowed not just the sinking of the carrier outside the Exclusion Zone, but the sinking of any Argentine warship regardless of the range of its weapons?

Apparently he could not even remember the timing of the

telephone call! Whether it was before or after he left Washington
for New York where he was to meet Perez de Cuellar, the U.N.
Secretary General — he did not know! Nor did he think it was
relevant as it was, 'one of many changes of Rules of Engagement
made in the course of the war!'

Because of Francis Pym's statement to the Foreign Affairs
Committee on 11 June 1984, Baroness Young, Minister of State
at the Foreign Office, when appearing before the Committee nine
days later, was asked to provide a list of the changes of Rules of
Engagement. This request was to lead eventually to the trial of
Clive Ponting. She was also asked the time that Francis Pym was
informed about the Chequers Sunday lunchtime change of Rules
of Engagement. Her reply is to be found on page 134 of the
Report, and reads that a telephone call was made between 9 a.m.
and 10 a.m. Washington time (1300 — 1400 G.M.T.) on 2nd
May, that is at the start of Francis Pym's morning talk with
Alexander Haig. And in spite of this he is reported as telling Haig
that no further escalation was imminent!

It is interesting to note that the Clarification Statement had to
be further clarified. Several South American countries protested
that to attack Argentine ships more than 12 nautical miles from
the Argentine coast would mean that they could be attacked within
the River Plate estuary and this violated the 1973 River Plate
Treaty and carried British aggression into the heart of the
continent, affecting Uruguayan territory as well as Argentinian.
This provoked a response at the United Nations from Sir Anthony
Parsons stating that the United Kingdom Government had
informed Uruguay that in spite of the statement of 7th May they
would not attack within 12 miles of that part of the coast between
the points Punta del Este and Punta Cabot San Antonio.

Here was a definite pointer to the fact that although the greatest
'threat to the mission' of our forces in the South Atlantic and
therefore covered by the warning of the 23rd April, came from
aircraft based in Argentina; the Attorney General, Sir Michael
Havers' advice had been that attack on the mainland or within
territorial waters would be very difficult to justify in International
Law as self-defence. Admiral Lewin explained this in an interview
given to Arthur Gavshon and Desmond Rice and reported in the
Guardian, 28th January 1985.

This would appear to be in direct contradiction to Sir Michael
Havers' later advice to Margaret Thatcher that the United States
air attack on Libya in response to terrorist activities not fully
proven, was in accordance with Article 51 — a decision that was
challenged by most legal experts, but as with the Belgrano decision
never ruled upon by any authoritative body.

We come then to the question that hangs over the deaths of 368 men. Why was the decision taken to change the Rules of Engagement allowing the sinking of all Argentine warships in International waters taken so hurriedly, and without prior consultation with the Mandarins, at lunchtime at Chequers on 2nd May?

Does the clue lie within James Prior's recent disclosures in his book 'A Balance of Power' in which he states that if Galtieri had accepted the Peruvian Peace Plan we would have had to go along with them and this would have split the Conservative Party? Which in turn, brings into question did Margaret Thatcher know nothing at all of the Peruvian Peace Plan as she claimed in May 1983? Why did the Peruvians think that Downing Street did know? What if any, was the role of her adviser Lord Hugh Thomas, the Chairman of the Centre for Policy Studies? Why did the Foreign Affairs Committee not persist with this line of inquiry?

Finally I would like to attempt to be constructive and to prevent the United Nation's good name being taken in vain. When countries try to gain respectability for their aggressive acts by claiming that they are acting under United Nations Article 51, could not a ruling be made by the United Nations that such claims will *automatically* be investigated and judgement pronounced on them by the International Court of Justice?

Clive Ponting
I think we start from the fact that there had been a cover-up over the circumstances surrounding the sinking and that's important because although Tam has talked about Westlands and so on, it's still a pretty rare event for the British Government that there's been a systematic attempt to mislead the House of Commons over a period as long as two years on an issue as important as this. So the question must arise, why?

Now I think there are two explanations. One of them is of course that all along they did know about the Peruvian Peace Plan and they sank the Belgrano anyway deliberately to scupper it. On that accusation I think we have to say at the moment there isn't enough evidence to prove it one way or the other.

The other explanation as to why they did it, and it could be that both explanations are right, is that they had deliberately misled both Parliament and the British public and indeed the United Nations as to the reasons and the type of strategy that they were actually adopting in the South Atlantic. Because right from the start on the 2nd April British action was justified under Article 51 and that we were not at war with Argentina. And as Diana has said this limits the amount of military action you can take. And therefore in terms of public opinion and world opinion it was very important for the British Government to try and sustain the line that it was Britain that was reacting to aggression by Argentina, that all of British actions were therefore extremely limited and designed to deal with specific and immediate Argentine threats and were carefully graduated in terms of raising military stakes whilst giving the Argentines an opportunity to negotiate. That was the official public position. And indeed if you look at the start of the war that's what seemed to be going on. There were negotiations in train and then on the 12th April the Maritime Exclusion Zone was set up treating as hostile Argentine warships on the surface within 200 miles of the Falklands, which could by that time be enforced by British nuclear submarines.

Then on the 23rd April we get what has been used since by the Government as the justification for all subsequent actions. It was a public warning put out that any approach by any Argentine military forces to the Task Force might be treated as hostile. The reason that the warning was made was that as the Task Force sailed south from Ascension Island it had been shadowed by Argentine civil aircraft to establish its position. Under the Rules of Engagement the military were unable to shoot down Argentine civil Electra aircraft. They put up a case to ministers that this could not be allowed to continue and therefore a warning was issued. The warning of course was also useful for the forthcoming invasion of South Georgia where different Rules of Engagement had to be applied than elsewhere in the South Atlantic.

On the 28th April the Government announced that there would be a Total Exclusion Zone around the Falklands covering both surface warships, submarines and aircraft coming into effect on the 30th. And this is what is interesting, that throughout this period the public warnings precede a change in the Rules of Engagement and precede the setting up of tighter and larger military actions. All this time it could be seen that what the Government was trying to do in public terms was to give the Argentines a chance to negotiate, whilst gradually upping the military stakes as British military forces got to the Falklands. A position that could be presented as reasonable both to the British public and to world opinion.

What happened on the 30th April immediately after the setting up of the Total Exclusion Zone was the discussion in the War Cabinet as to what the next steps of the military operations were to be. And the military made a very strong case that the Argentine aircraft carrier should be sunk because with its range of aircraft it could naturally pose a threat to the Task Force from a considerable distance outside the Exclusion Zone. A reasonable military case, but the question is what were the Government going to do? They had the option to do what they had always done and issue a public warning beforehand to the Argentines that this is indeed what would take place unless the aircraft carrier retreated out of range. They chose not to do that but to make a decision instead to sink without warning the aircraft carrier if H.M.S. Splendid which was then believed to be shadowing the aircraft carrier could carry out the attack.

That evening Francis Pym met Michael Havers, the Attorney General, together with the senior Foreign Office legal adviser. They came to the view that under Article 51 it would, in Whitehall language, be extremely difficult to justify publicly what the British had done, if indeed the carrier had been sunk without warning, that it would put Britain in an invidious position. Now, I think you have to realise how Whitehall Minutes are written. It would have to be an extremely brave Foreign Secretary and Attorney-General that told the Prime Minister that what she was doing was illegal under International Law. There are other ways of phrasing it and this was one of them. In effect it asked her to think again. The Minute was sent on the 1st May and at no time was any consideration ever given to it. It is admitted that the War Cabinet never discussed it and it was simply put on one side. So in other words the Prime Minister decided to ignore the advice of the Government's senior legal officer and the Foreign Secretary, pointing out the difficult position they were in. Because at any time on that day the aircraft carrier could have been sunk. It was only because H.M.S. Splendid lost contact with the carrier and couldn't find it again that the attack never took place.

On the 2nd May the Government took another decision to sink any Argentine ship outside Argentine territorial waters without any warning. Again by implication, the very arguments that Havers and Pym had put the day before on sinking the aircraft carrier applied yet again to this decision. Because it could be argued that the Government was no longer saying there was an immediate military threat, it was simply going to sink anything outside Argentine territorial waters.

Then on the 4th May John Nott had to stand up and justify what the Government had done. I think it's important to remember that there was a great deal of world opinion which was concerned about the way that the Belgrano had been sunk and this is before the retaliation on the Sheffield. Therefore Nott was determined to paint a picture that the Belgrano had been an immediate threat to the Task Force and that is why I believe he took the decision to try to paint the picture that it had only been detected at 8 o'clock, virtually on top of the Task Force, by a submarine and the commander had therefore taken the decision to sink it. Of course the facts were very different. But that looked like a convincing justification.

Now since 1982 the Government have always said that the warning of the 23rd April covered the sinking of the Belgrano. Well, if it did, neither the Attorney General nor the Foreign Secretary thought it did on the 1st May. And if it did why did the Government issue another warning on the 7th May saying exactly what it was they were intending to do and in fact had decided to do five days before? — that is sink Argentine warships outside of territorial waters.

So I think there is a case for saying that the Government itself was at best unsure and extremely dubious that what they had done, when they saw the consequences of it, was indeed legal, and that that was one of the main reasons for the subsequent cover up. And it may be that Peru was another reason on top but I think it shows that it's not just people outside of Whitehall who felt that the action might be illegal in International Law. It was actually the very people inside Whitehall whose job it was to advise the Government about International Law who had exactly the same doubts.

Eric Ogden
Fellow dissenters, I think that's a fair term, many questions have been asked about the Belgrano, some questions have been answered but there are always more claims, more myths put forward. My purpose is to suggest that there is no true mystery about the sinking of the Belgrano and my purpose in the time I would want to take is to try to refute just three of the claims.

If you will look at page 11 of the Belgrano Handbook, number 6 on the right hand side, 'No British lives had been lost prior to the sinking.' That is a statement of the fact. But there is the inference that because lives were lost in the Belgrano and consequentially, it was the sinking of the Belgrano that had been the cause and effect of the loss of life in the Falklands War, and I want to refute this suggestion.

The suggestion is made that the Belgrano had special exemptions from the normal rules of war, and I want to suggest that in practical terms the Belgrano had no special exemption from the normal rules of war. She was simply one ship, part of a three force group operating around one part of the Falkland Islands, whilst other fleets, almost all of the ships of the Argentine navy were operating towards the north and she was simply part of an overall combined operation by the Argentine navy against the ships of the Royal Navy.

I want to suggest that the decision to attack the Belgrano was taken for the security of the British Task Force and there is no justification for any other claims that it was primarily a political decision and not a military one.

So to take those three claims in order if I may. The Falkland War was begun by the government of Argentina without any formalities or ultimatum, when that government was still engaged in diplomatic discussions with the British Government on the future sovereignty of the Islands. At that date, the 2nd April 1982, the Falklands had been under the control, the sovereignty of Britain and the British administration, had been governed for 147 years by a British administration under British sovereignty from a date which preceeded the establishment of the State of Argentina. This morning I heard people saying, well there is some perhaps doubt about the validity of Britain's claims of sovereignty. If 7 years give people squatters' rights, 147 years recognition of International Law would seem a reasonable case of the sovereignty. The British Administratiron and Sovereignty of the Falklands was recognised by custom and practice, by every maritime nation, by the United Nations, by International Law and by every country in the world, except of course Argentina. And on the morning of the 2nd April 1982 the combined forces of the Argentine navy, army and airforce led by their best commanders and made up of their most skilled and professional forces invaded the Falklands. With more than 6,000 invaders opposed to less than 100 defenders, that was a total of 69 Royal Marines and some 20 part-time volunteers of the Falkland Islands Defence Force, it's not surprising that resistance to the invasion ceased after a few hours when the defenders were very properly ordered to surrender by the commanding officer on the instructions of the Governor. That was a wholly proper decision to have taken.

Now much is made of the fact that's referred to in part 6, that the invasion and occupation of the Island was carried through without loss of life. The Junta claimed that their forces had taken great care to ensure that no British lives were lost during the invasion. And the facts in fact refute such a claim.

The shooting war of the Falklands began at 0608 on the morning of the 2nd April when a force of 100 men of the Buzo Tactica, that's the Argentine equivalent of the British Special Boat Squadron, attacked the Royal Marine barracks at Moody Brook near Stanley in a classic house-clearance exercise. The words are misleading. No warnings were given, no calls for surrender were made and the barracks were systematically, professionally, attacked and destroyed by grenades, rifles, machine guns, every room was shattered by phosphorous grenades and riddled with bullets. The attack on Moody Brook barracks was intended to destroy the defenders. I saw the results of that attack in February 1983, the evidence was there for anyone to see. No defender could have survived such an attack. Fortunately those barracks had been abandoned on the instruction of the commanding officer of the Marines and the Marines who the Argentinian troops thought were there were in fact at Government House. Had they been there then British casualities would have been at least every Marine who was in those barracks. In contrast, the attack on Government House was not meant to destroy the defenders but to force their surrender. Government House lies below a high ridge in an isolated position between the ridge and the waters of Stanley harbour. Given that it was the seat of government it was the most undefendable position in the whole of the Islands. I suggest that this enquiry might be well advised, perhaps better occupied asking why Government House was defended rather than why the Belgrano was sunk. That's one of the questions I've never got a proper answer to yet. I do know that the instructions given to the Governor then were different to the instructions given to his predecessors and I'm still trying to find out why. But whatever the reason was that no British lives were taken during the invasion, it was a fortunate accident of history and had no part in the intentions or operations of the Argentine invaders. So the claim that is inferred, not only in this document but many, that casualties only began because we sank the Belgrano doesn't in fact stand up to the facts of the invasion.

Now to turn to the Belgrano. The Belgrano was at sea on the 2nd May with two escort ships, the Piedra Buena and the Hipolito Bouchard, part of a combined operation of almost the whole of the Argentine navy aimed against the British Task Force. The Belgrano and her two escorting vessels were sighted, observed and followed by the British submarine for at least 30 hours. It is as though the lady on the camera in the centre (in the hall) was sitting in the middle of the Falkland Islands, the Belgrano and her escorts were coming round the south, somewhere over the back was Admiral Woodward, and the Argentine forces were going there. A classic 'look, find, search and destroy.' No one seems to have enquired why the Belgrano and her escorts were not the ancient useless little force that is sometimes suggested. Her age is correct, but this particular booklet doesn't say that she was armed with anti-submarine weapons, that she had two helicopters. It doesn't mention, but Mr Ponting has mentioned, the Exocets on the escorts. The Belgrano with her escorts ought to have been a formidable force. If we ask why the Belgrano was attacked, we should also ask how it was that the Belgrano and two destroyers didn't discover the Conqueror during the 30 hours she was observing them. I would suggest that the Belgrano was attacked because she was a danger to the submarine and a threat to every ship in the British Task Force seeking the liberation of the Falklands. The Belgrano was sunk because the professional skills of her commander were less than the professional skills of the commander of the British submarine. The attack was made from this British submarine with two Second World War gas-propelled torpedoes of a vintage Mark 8 model which had a range of less than 4,500 yards. Professional sailors on the Belgrano and her escorts ought to have detected the submarine and taken some offensive action against them if they had been doing their job. So the Enquiry might like to enquire why in fact they seem to have done nothing to defend the Belgrano, nothing to attack the British submarine after the attack was made.

The Belgrano was afloat for two hours after she was hit, the sea conditions were normal for the seas at that time of year, and the loss of 321, those are Ministry of Defence figures, I'll accept your figure of 368....

Diana Gould: That is the figure....

Eric Ogden: But I'll accept it, of up to 400. The total loss of life from the Belgrano was much greater than could have been incurred immediately from the impact of those two torpedoes. So the total loss of life must have been as much due to the incompetence of the Argentine commanders on both the Belgrano and the destroyers as it was to the impact of the torpedoes.

I've sailed those waters in the south west Atlantic, admittedly a long time ago, I won't say just how long ago, admittedly on a merchant ship armed only with a four-inch gun and a couple of bofors. We were trying to get round by Cape Horn from the Atlantic into the Pacific. Someone was waiting there to make it difficult for us. We went up towards the Falklands, that was the first time I saw the Falklands, and eventually sneaked through the Straits of Magellan and got into comparative safety. So I know something about that. I know at the time that for sailors at least and for situations of war, of hostilities, formal declarations of war or hostilities are not universal. The practical rules of war change very little, and I would suggest and I think there is a sailor over there wearing the South Atlantic medal, I don't know what his experience is, he can tell us. I would suspect that every sailor on every ship in time of war knows that his ship is in danger from and a threat to every other ship in the opposing force and that he is at risk from them. Sailors don't draw lines on charts. Sailors leave that to landbased lawyers. Go areas or no-go areas have little part in the feelings and views of most sailors. I would have suggested

that no one on the Belgrano would have thought they were safe
from attack because they were on one side of a supposed line or
the other. Any more than a sailor in the Bismarck would have
thought he was safe simply because he was heading home, rather
than away.

Diana Gould: There was a war then.

Eric Ogden: I'm making the point! Whether it is technically a
war or not a war, whether it is a declaration or not, from Pearl
Harbour all through history war has been a practical one regardless
of the finer print or the circumstances in which it was happening.
And the whole of naval warfare from Drake to Dunkirk, from
Trafalgar to Trondheim, from the Mediterranean to the River
Plate and Medway denies any such assumptions. Everyone on the
Belgrano must have know she was liable to be attacked at any
time just as they ought to have been ready to be able to attack
anyone else at any time.

May I make one personal comment at this particular time,
particularly because it is Remembrance time. We hear from time
to time, we hear specially now, of those who gave their lives. There
may be some, very brave, very few, courageous people who
deliberately take an act which is going to lose them their lives, but
for most of us.... all right so I speak for myself, I was in the
Merchant Navy when three out of four ships out of Liverpool were
sunk and never came back again. We always hoped it would
happen to somebody else. So there is sacrifice, there is risk. But
I get a little sick when somebody says you were prepared to
sacrifice your life. I take what credit I can for what I did do but I
hoped it would happen to somebody else, and a little reality like
that does no harm. It takes nothing away from the courage or
bravery of our sailors. The same applies to every man or woman
in any part of the Services. And will you remember that it was an
Argentine admiral not a British commander who said publicly after
the sinking of the Belgrano, 'The Belgrano was a danger to any
British ship around the Falklands. The British had not only the
right but the duty to try and sink her.' And that came from an
admiral in the Argentine Navy not from a British source.

Now finally I want to turn as quickly as I can to consider the
claims, the myths that the attack on the Belgrano was ordered for
primarily political purposes not naval ones and to destroy any
chance of a peaceful solution of the conflict and in particular to
destroy the Peruvian Initiative.

I happen to have been in Parliament during the time. I happen
to have been one of those nearly 20 or 30 who actually knew where
the Falklands were before the invasion. If they'd taken any notice
of the advice one or two of us gave to the Foreign Office prior to

1981 there may not have been an invasion. It certainly was the avoidable war. And let me also add that the Falklands is one of the few things with which I happen to agree with this Government but that is what we're talking about today. From the Argentine invasion of the Falklands on the 2nd April the United Nations had ordered the Argentine government to withdraw its forces from the Falklands and the Junta did not remove its troops, indeed they reinforced them to a total of more than 10,000. The front of this well-prepared leaflet, quotes I think on page 3,

'It is, however, becoming increasingly clear that General Galtieri's invasion was so flagrant and foolish an affront to international order that he could almost certainly have been evicted, without blood-shed, through the United Nations or by some alternative means,....'

The simple fact is that a month went by from the invasion and no-one had been able to remove him. So what are these alternative means? They weren't working then, he'd gone exactly opposite. So that was hope not the experience. Between the 2nd April, the invasion, and the 2nd May at least five possible alternative peaceful solutions were put for the peaceful resolution from the United Nations, from General Haig, three British solutions and the Peruvian one with various combinations. One of the difficulties of understanding the British point of view is that there were in fact two, there was Mrs Thatcher and her closer friends saying one thing and there was Francis Pym saying something quite different, probably within ten minutes of making a joint statement in the House of Commons. So some of the confusion arises from that diversion of opinion. But every one of those proposals including the British one, included the fact that the Argentinian forces would withdraw, the British Task Force would come back at least to Gibraltar and further back, and there would be a neutral Administration, a suspension of the British Administration and a netral Administration in the Islands consisting in the main of an Argentine Commissioner, a United Nations Commissioner and a British Commissioner — a neutral Administration, while efforts were made to obtain a peaceful solution to the sovereignty issue.

The Argentine Commissioner would have claimed equal rights for the Islanders for Argentine settlers, the majority of the British Falkland Islanders would have left the Islands with or without compensation. Argentine settlers would have come in, bought land, built new settlements and within a very short time a majority of Argentinian-born Falkland Islanders would have been demanding the re-unification of the Islands. I understood that, the Islanders understood that, friends of the Islanders here understood it. I don't know whether Mrs Thatcher understood it but I'm certain that Francis Pym understood it but it would have got him off the hook.

The consequences of the Peruvian Initiative would have been essentially the same as any other, including the points put forward by the British Government. So why should the British sink the Belgrano to destroy an initiative which was essentially the same as their own, any one of their own? General Galtieri and his government didn't recognise any of the options that were passed out to them. They could have had the Falklands on a plate. Costa Mendez did, but was overruled, but unfortunately the Junta rejected it. As I say Argentina began the Falklands War because of the ambitions and illusions of the Junta and generals. They lost the Falklands War because of military incompetence and incompetence of the generals and Junta. The casualties of the Belgrano were part of that incompetence. I suggest there's no real mystery about the sinking of the Belgrano and to pretend that there is doesn't help the cause of democracy in Argentina. There are other questions about the Falklands which are still to be asked and answered but for this one, whilst I agree wholeheartedly the Falklands was the *avoidable war of every war that has ever been*, ask other questions, try to get other answers, but leave the Belgrano in peace.

John Ferguson: I wonder if I might make just two observations and then a couple of questions. The observations are, I would like also to say that I'm very grateful that we have heard Eric Ogden. I had a feeling when I looked at the documentation that for reasons outside the planning and the people who planned this, I do know that, we were hearing one side predominantly....

Diana Gould: We did invite all the people in the War Cabinet, everybody we could, asked Mrs Thatcher if she would send a representative because we couldn't expect her to come, but those who replied said that they had given evidence to the Foreign Affairs Committee which is why we feel we can use that evidence — they're standing by it. I would just like to say that neither Mrs Thatcher nor Sir John Nott even acknowledged any of the three communications we sent them, not even an acknowledgement of receipt.

John Ferguson: Thank you very much. And the other issue, I'll just briefly comment, I don't know whether I ought to but Diana raised the matter of a possible consultation of the International Court of Justice when Article 51 is invoked. The International Court of Justice will take about two years to come to a decision, therefore it is actually impractical in any given situation in order to take it post hoc or before anything is going to emerge, in a situation it is actually impractical.

Two questions, one I think probably to Clive Ponting. I think the puzzle that I have had in reading this relates to the question of the Rules of Engagement and whether the Belgrano could reasonably expect to be attacked. And Eric Ogden said that of course she could reasonably expect to be attacked. Now in the evidence to the Foreign Affairs Committee it was stated by Lord Lewin that the Rules of Engagement are a secret document and therefore in a sense there is no warning. There is the confusion between the definition of the Total Exclusion Zone which I understand the commander of the Belgrano said that he thought the Total Exclusion Zone meant that outside the Exclusion Zone you were reasonably safe. Or is the document of April 23rd to be taken really as in International Law a reasonable warning. And I think this is the major case. Were the Government really under the impression that they were giving a reasonable warning, in which case the 7th May definition is a realisation that they hadn't defined it properly?

Clive Ponting: I think as you say this goes to the nub of the whole question. Rules of Engagement are certainly secret documents in which what rules are operating for the Navy at any time are going to be kept secret in the middle of a war. But the important point is how they relate to the public warnings that had been given under Article 51. Eric was saying it didn't matter where it was because the Bismarck would have been sunk anywhere on the high seas. Yes, of course it would, because Britain and Germany were at war at the time and nobody bothered about territorial waters and bombing the mainland in the Second World War. We were not at war with Argentina. We were actually under Article 51, as Carrington had made plain right from the evening of the invasion.

The point is that apart from the period from the 30th April to 7th May the Rules of Engagement for Naval ships were either the same as or more restricted than the public warnings that had been issued to Argentina as to what military action we would take. Obviously it's quite reasonable for the politicians to issue a public warning, but actually ensure that the Navy take even less action than they've said they would take in public because they want to continue with the diplomatic activity. So that for example until the 30th April no Naval ship was allowed to attack Argentine warships outside of the Exclusion Zone. The Total Exclusion Zone was only set up on the 30th April, yet within two hours of setting it up the Government had decided to take action that extended it. And the crucial point is they did not issue a public warning. As far as the Argentines were concerned action was still restricted to within the Exclusion Zone. And that indeed was the public position that the British Government was taking. Pym, on the 1st

May after he'd written, with Havers, a Minute of dissent about what the War Cabinet had decided, was still saying at a press conference in America after the attacks on Port Stanley, that no action was contemplated by the British other than to enforce the Exclusion Zone.

What had happened was of course that on the 30th April and the 2nd May the Government had taken decisions that significantly extended the military action that the Navy was allowed to take, but without giving any public warning that this is what they had done until the 7th May. I do not think that the 23rd April warning could be used to cover the action because if it did, all the 23rd April warning in effect says is that they would attack Argentine ships anyway. In that case why did they announce on the 30th April the Total Exclusion Zone and why on the 7th May did they go for a formal public warning outside territorial waters? So their actions at the time don't sustain the case about the 23rd April warning. They've used it subsequently I believe as the best justification they'd got for what they did.

John Ferguson: Thank you very much. Could I just ask a double question to Eric Ogden. You've made the case for what happened. The first part is, if Britain were going to invoke Article 51, ought there not to have been a far stronger military presence in the Falklands long before or are we to say that the Intelligence Services were incompetent? That's the other possibility. The second part defended the sinking of the Belgrano as normal military activity. Why was it not sunk when it was steaming towards the Exclusion Zone, but was sunk when it had been steaming away for 11 hours? This is a totally open question, it's a puzzle to me.

Eric Ogden: The first one sir, I believe the British Intelligence Services were wholly good. At one time I had the impression that the only person earning his money in the British Embassy in Buenos Aires was the chauffeur and he of course was Argentinian. But their intelligence information was good. The night before the invasion we had picked up some talk about the Argentine manoeuvres. At 11 o'clock that night I asked Francis Pym if he had a statement to make that things would go worse before they became better. Would he make it quite clear that the resources at our disposal were much greater than Argentina might think, would he guarantee to recall Parliament? Everything but say, will you say publicly that you know they're under way to the Argentinians? At that time Pym had been talking, and Mrs Thatcher had been talking, to Haig and President Reagan, but privately. I still believe that if the British Government had announced publicly that they had been told by their intelligence sources that Argentine fleets were heading for the Falklands, and if the Argentines came within 50 miles of the Falklands coast it would be considered an act of war, then the Argentines would have had the way of coming round. But that wasn't done. So the war was avoidable. Costa Mendez had been given every indication that Britain wanted to get rid of it, from Endurance and everything else. My first visit on behalf of Nicholas Ridley to the Islands was in 1981. We gave a report back and if they'd taken the slightest bit of notice of it, it would have made clear. It was the avoidable war.

The Belgrano, the sinking: I don't know why it took 30 hours from the first sighting of the Belgrano to its sinking. I do know it shows that there are dangers and perhaps stupidities in trying to conduct a war by civilians from a distance of 8,000 miles. I think in practical terms you have to give freedom of operation to your commanders or fire them. But I still say whichever way she was going we were entitled to sink her. What I do find difficult to accept, the restrictions that the British Government placed on our own services in the way that they said, if your forces are within the 200 miles then they're open to attack. A plane can come in and sink the Sheffield and we will chase her all the way to the 200 mies and then come back. I think that was not the way that wars can or could be fought. I think the fact that they could come in from their land bases, attack our forces and then be safe back again was a nonsense in any military terms at all. We didn't do it in any other war. We couldn't say, all right half way across the channel you're at risk, once you get back to Calais you're safe, so it was a nonsense, made a nonsense of the whole operation. But that was their restriction. That was the kind of thing that put our troops at risk, not the Argentines.

Diana Gould: The answer I gave you originally to your last question was that in Lewin's own words "there was not a war." It is in his evidence. But I would like to make an addition: the fact that it states in our handbook the truth that no British lives had been lost prior to the sinking, that stands as it stands and I'm not arguing with anybody about whether it was fortuitous. I think probably it was very good fortune that none of those Royal Marines were killed. But I would just like to remind Eric Ogden that those marines were repatriated and came back and fought with the Task Force. That gives a slant to it.

The other thing I would like to take exception to, Eric Ogden says how incompetent the Argentinian Navy was but we have it on good authority that the Conqueror according to the Sethia diary for instance, after they'd sunk the cruiser, they were attacked, depth charges were dropped on them, so that is another point. So it isn't true to say that they didn't attack the Conqueror.

The answer to the question again, why were they incompetent? I did write a little monograph which I entitled the 'Unfortunate Admiral' because I do think that if you take Lord Lewin's evidence he does tend to contradict himself rather a lot. And I would like to have asked him a question had he come here about the fact that the Belgrano and her escorts ploughed a straight furrow, they did not zigzag. Now Eric Ogden was actually in the Merchant Navy in the last war and would know the way the convoy zigzagged, or their escorts zigzagged. I mean if you are aware of the fact that you could be sunk at any moment, you take these precautions. The Argentinians were definitely aware of the fact that our submarines, our nuclear powered submarines were down in their waters by April 13th. So Captain Bonzo had no excuse in not knowing that he was likely to have a submarine on his tail. So of course you come to the question, why the heck didn't he zigzag? Why didn't he take these precautionary measures? And the only answer to that, Eric Ogden, is that because he thought he was in such a position he did not think he was a threat and therefore he thought that he was in International waters and was entitled to be there and did not need to take any precautionary actions. So that answers some of your queries.

Just one other thing: the Argentine Admiral, I'm not sure which one you're quoting, who said that we had every right to sink them — I understood that on a Panorama programme an Argentine Admiral said 'We would have done the same'. He then later on clarified this; he said it was taken out of context. And my understanding was that he was referring to the captain of the Conqueror, he would have obeyed orders. The captain of the Conqueror, Commander Wreford-Brown, was given the orders, the change of the Rules of Engagement, which meant that he would have been breaking orders if he hadn't sunk it, or attacked it and would have been therefore liable to court-martial.

Eric Ogden: Can I say quite simply any commander of any ship, Merchant or Navy, in those circumstances round the Falklands, if he really believed that he was setting out as part of a combined force round here to attack the British ships, British Navy over there, but it was perfectly all right to doodle along quite happily until he got within 200 miles, then he was liable to be attacked because of something on a piece of paper. He wasn't doing his duty in my opinion. Anybody on any ship when there's any fighting going on anywhere, has to protect his own ship and be prepared to sink or be sunk. And do you think that the Argentines would have been having this form of Enquiry if in fact when the

Conqueror tried to sink him she'd failed and the Belgrano had sunk the Conqueror? The Belgrano went down because she didn't take those elementary precautions.

Diana Gould: That would have been an act of self-defence if the Conqueror had tried to sink and then had not sunk the Belgrano, it of course would have been entitled under Article 51 to defend itself.

Eric Ogden: Nobody on those ships was running around saying 'I've got the Article 51 under my shirt, I'm perfectly all right.'

Richard Baker: Briefly I think I already understand this but I want to get it absolutely clear. Am I to understand that the Attorney-General advised the Government in writing that the attack on an aircraft carrier would be against International Law and the Government ignored that? Again when the question of attacking any ship arose, that the orders to attack the Belgrano were given, am I right in thinking that no further advice from the Attorney-General was sought?

Clive Ponting: On the last question you're absolutely right. On the 2nd May, as far as we were able to find out, I'm not sure even whether Havers was present at Chequers that day. If he was, there is no evidence that he was consulted or gave any advice about the legality of the decision to sink any Argentine warship on the high seas. It's not sure he was consulted or even knew about the decision before it was implemented. The question of what he actually said on the 30th April, the Minute that he wrote appeared in the Observer just after my trial, it was signed formally by the Foreign Secretary Pym. What he actually says is drafted in Whitehall language saying, 'After discussing with the Attorney-General the way in which our action would have to be publicly justified and its legality defended, I believe our position would be immeasurably strengthened if we had given a warning to the Argentine Government.' Now what that actually means in Whitehall language is, that I am advising you that in effect this action is not legally justified under International Law without a warning.

Richard Baker: Finally I'd like to ask another question of Eric Ogden. He spoke of apprehension in the Islands immediately before the attack took place. Could I ask him whether there was apprehension in the Islands at any time earlier than the vital attack and if so what representations were made to the Government? Was it only just before, or were the people on the Islands concerned about an attack earlier than that and did they make representations that they would like to be defended or anything like that?

Eric Ogden: My Association was formed from 1968 when the

British Government seemed to be making moves for handing the sovereignty of the Falklands over to Argentina. The Association was set up to defend British Falkland Islanders' points of view and to represent them here. We've moved on from that. We're no longer just delegates of the Falkland Islands. So it was a political Association. My first visit was in 1981, to follow our Parliamentary Association partly at the request of Nicholas Ridley to find out what impressions his own visit in 1980 had made, the propositions he'd made to them. The Islanders had been concerned about possible invasion from the time a few years before when a Private Enterprise invasion took place for Condor. They have good communications, it's a great place for rumour but they have good communcations. And there were occasions when every time the Argentine Navy went out for exercises it was on its way to the Falklands to an invasion. The Marines were some 43 in number and then increased to some 68 or 86. They were armed with a few rifles, a couple of machine guns, no not even a machine gun. They hadn't even got an inflatable dinghy. They had no radar. Their communications equipment was like carrying two 10-ton car batteries around. They used the local communications of the Islands. We asked John Nott to give them at least some walkie-talkies and that was under consideration by the time of the invasion. They increased the force from 43 up to 86. Useless.

Richard Baker: They didn't ask for .... for their own protection?

Eric Ogden: It would have needed thousands and we couldn't even get them walkie-talkies, or a dinghy, or a helicopter, or a radar set in the west. We had just lost Endurance. They had no light aircraft.

Richard Baker: You protested about this?

Eric Ogden: Yes, this was protested. Those were made consistently and the only real protection would have been to say, "We are not going to negotiate the transfer. It is British sovereignty, it is ours and if you take it we'll come in and kick you out again."

Malcolm Dando: I've got an intervention which I think we ought to take. It's from Mr Makin an Argentinian journalist.

Dr G.A. Makin: It's factual, general evidence both from a departmental enquiry and an office court-martial.... It gave the reason of an operational nature why the Belgrano was there and I just wanted to give the reasons of a military nature for the presence of the Belgrano. The High Command, in papers that the Foreign Affairs Committee had the chance to see in full, came to the conclusion that the Argentine Navy was unable to face British ships one-to-one and that the only opportunity in which it had a reasonable chance would be when the British Navy was engaged in trying to support the landings. And that circumstance in the point of view of the Argentine High Command had presented itself as from the bombardment, both air and naval, of Port Stanley. So that was the reason for movement of the three Argentine Task Forces on to the Island, closing in, and as the presence of the Belgrano was the third of these forces it was there as a tripwire. It was acknowledged that it wasn't, shall we say, the most efficient of ships from the military point of view but it was always able to be a useful trip wire and that was the reason for it being posted outside the Exclusion Zone at times. That was all I wanted to say at this time.

Wade Tidbury: Referring to Eric Ogden's line about sailors' feelings and ideas concerning the Rules of Engagement, I know that our officers on our ship, the Alacrity, took very, very seriously the Rules of Engagement. We *did* draw lines on charts, we did have charts in our operations room on the Alacrity, drawn out showing the Exclusion Zone and to suggest to the Enquiry that the Navy wasn't taking this seriously or taking it as something which should be respected by both sides, is something which I disagree with. The Alacrity was involved in the bombing of, if I can just use this (Refers to chart on wall) as it's quite convenient, the area around Port Stanley. The encampments were bombed with shrapnel shells as I said earlier. The Belgrano was here, the rest of the Task Force was over here. This is reasonably accurate even though it's just been drawn up on a chart....

Diana Gould: It's based on the Ministry of Defence chart which was supplied to the Foreign Affairs Committee.

Wade Tidbury: There are some things which I'd like to point out. We were detailed at 1500 hours, one hour after the Belgrano had been sighted, to leave the main group and carry out the bombings of the Island's Argentine encampments, not the airfield as you have been told: it was the Argentine encampments which we bombed with shrapnel shells. Now you may just say that that was in consequence of war. I say that it was something that sticks in my gut to this day, the fact that we were maiming people and the British people were being told.... Was it coincidence that it was just one hour after the Belgrano had been sighted that we were being told to do this? I suggest it isn't. I suggest that it was a co-ordinated plan to sink any peace plans. The only point on this chart that I would disagree with , because I did see the charts on the Alacrity, that this point here where it came slightly downwards it was slightly going upwards, perhaps in a Northerly direction, but away from the Falkland Islands towards the Argentine mainland and outside of the Exclusion Zone. Now it wasn't until the sinking of the Sheffield that our aircraft actually ventured outside this area. So that your suggestion again that once we'd been attacked we would not have chased them outside the area is something again I completely disagree with. And constantly our ships were going outside the Exclusion Zone to refuel and I would suggest that it was perhaps more in this direction, it would be that much safer considering the air attacks which resulted in the sinking of the Sheffield. They are just a few of the points I'd like to point out.

The other thing that I would also like to bring up was the point you made about sovereignty. If this country actually held the sovereignty so dear to the Falkland Islanders why is it that amendments had to be made to a bill in Parliament just after the Falklands war because 25% of the Falkland Island population were going to be refused the right to be British citizens?

Eric Ogden: It wasn't just the right of the British citizens, the 25% were not recognised as British citizens because their grandparents hadn't been born in this country, so they were denied the right of patriation. That was a stupid mistake, but it was done by this Government simply because they were afraid of the consequences for Hong Kong. Later after the war they did what ought to have been done before.

Can I ask one question? Your positioning is absolutely right as I understand it. You probably know the story that Admiral Woodward was to get the Burma Star because the fleet was so far to the east that it was nearer Burma than it was the Falklands. But the defensive part. Agreed the commanders would try not to attack outside a certain area but surely your commanders of your ship, when you went down from wherever you were, the Mediterranean, didn't simply say, all right we can swan around until we get within a close particular range of the Falklands and then we are at risk. Your commanders wouldn't have done that surely? I'm saying that ought to have been done by the commanders of the Belgrano. After all the Argentinians did attack or try to attack Ascension, they did try to attack Gibraltar later I would think. Did nobody tell you?

Wade Tidbury: They tried to attack Gibraltar?

Eric Ogden: Oh yes, yes.

Clive Ponting: We never found any evidence of that inside the Ministry of Defence.

Eric Ogden: You picked up six lads in the dockyard, they were taken across to the airport and shipped back home again.

Wade Tidbury: How big an attack was there?

Eric Ogden: Six.

Wade Tidbury: There are about 4,000 troops approximately based on Gibraltar and you're saying that six....

Eric Ogden: Six tried to get through the dockyard.

Wade Tidbury: Are you trying to say the dockyard was under attack?

Eric Ogden: With what they were carrying it certainly was.

Wade Tidbury: What were they carrying?

Eric Ogden: Limpits. Information I have given you, check it. I say there are a lot of unanswered questions. There's one that you might like to follow through. There were attacks tried to be made much later both on Ascension and on Gibraltar. If you're talking about nuclear weapons let's see what there is in Argentina as well as in the old Sheffield.

Diana Gould: That chart on the wall is the chart that the Ministry of Defence was asked to supply to the Foreign Affairs Committee and you will find it in the Report. I have queried that final position because I am a geographer and if you have a bearing of 280 you're going north of west and you can all see it is going south west. I cannot explain it, but on page 184 of the Report you will find the signals that the Conqueror sent and the signals that she sent gave the latitude and the longitude of the sightings. The person who has made this chart, somebody in the Ministry of Defence, has simply plotted the points that they were given in the signals from the Conqueror and then joined them up with straight lines. And you will, if you look at those signals, find that the latitude of the sinking is definitely south of the latitude of the reversing point. Now I cannot explain that.

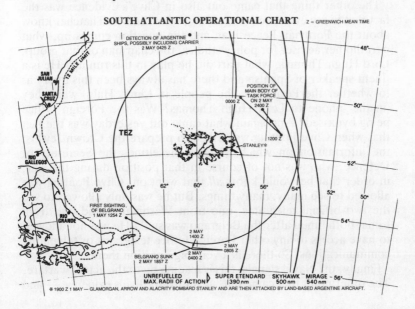

SOUTH ATLANTIC OPERATIONAL CHART   Z = GREENWICH MEAN TIME

V

The Political Costs of Sinking the Belgrano

Paul Rogers

Diana Gould
What I feel I have been asked to say will be to let the people here know today some of the facts that emerged very strongly yesterday which had not really been clarified before. One that came out from Clive Ponting's evidence very strongly, was that after the April 30th meeting of the War Cabinet with all their advisers at which the decision was taken to sink the Argentine aircraft carrier if it was found by a submarine, that the Foreign Secretary Francis Pym and the Attorney General Sir Michael Havers and their chief legal adviser, because they were disquieted and worried that it was not covered, or would not be seen to be covered by Article 51 in international opinion, sent a Minute to the Prime Minister's office. The important thing that came out yesterday was that the Minute was completely ignored, absolutely and completely ignored and our question is, why? Why was it never referred to, nothing done about it at all?

The other thing that came out also in Clive's evidence was the fact that in my evidence I was saying, what did Mrs Thatcher know about the Peruvian Peace Plan and the question comes up, what part did her adviser for policy studies, the chairman of that group, Lord Hugh Thomas, what part did he play in this run up? He is a fluent speaker of Spanish and there has always been this query as to whether the Peruvians, the people in Lima, Haig, were they on the 'phone to Lord Hugh Thomas? Was the Foreign Office being bypassed? And again what came out yesterday was the fact that when Clive Ponting was asked to prepare the Crown Jewels, the information on which Michael Heseltine, the Secretary of Defence, who was not of course in that position during the war, in order that he would know *all* that went on, Clive Ponting was allowed to see many, many things. But he was only allowed to see the two official telegrams, one from Washington and one from Lima, both timed after the Belgrano was sunk. He was not allowed to have access to any other Foreign Office telegrams or telephone communications. So there is a very big question there.

Finally, the Naval signals: this is leading on to the actual warfare. The other point that came out, again from Clive's evidence — and one must feel that as the person who prepared the whole report for the Ministry of Defence, I think we must accept that he does know what he's talking about — there came out the fact that there is a signal that was vital to the whole question that was omitted from this Foreign Affairs Committee Report. The Foreign Affairs Committee did request that the Ministry of Defence send them a list of the signals between Northwood, the headquarters which were running the war, and H.M.S. Conqueror, the nuclear powered submarine down in those waters of the South Atlantic shadowing the Belgrano. They asked for a summary of those signals and they got a summary of the signals between Northwood and Conqueror. I think one must realise that what you're up against all the time is that people will stick to exactly what you ask and won't enlarge on anything. So as a result in the Report, you will find on page 184 a list of the signals. I won't go through all of them but I'll start on the 2nd May although they actually start the day before because Conqueror then reported definitely sighting, not just thinking they'd got them but sighting, the whole Belgrano group. They reported that at 3 o'clock on the Saturday afternoon, but I'm not going to read that one out.

We come to the 2nd May. Now at 5 a.m. London Time, British Summer Time, H.M.S. Conqueror reports the Belgrano group and I'll just read it:

'55 degrees 20 minutes south, 60 degrees 14 west, course 90 degrees, speed 13 knots'

and the next signal that we get is as asked, signals between Conqueror and Northwood:

'10.15 a.m. (Summer Time here) Northwood instructs Conqueror that the Belgrano is not to be attacked until allowed by the Rules of Engagement.'

And following that of course we have Lord Lewin going to Chequers and getting the permission. But there is a signal missing in between those two and this came out in Clive's evidence. It has been said on television in the World in Action programme but it isn't in here and I think what Clive said now makes this official. At 8 o'clock on that Sunday morning, I think Northwood were astonished because they heard the signal from Admiral Sandy Woodward, head of the Task Force down in the Atlantic, whose signals all went via Northwood to whoever he was signalling, and they heard Admiral Woodward order the Conqueror to sink the Belgrano. Now that makes sense then of the 10.15 a.m. order from Northwood saying, 'Don't sink the Belgrano until we've changed the Rules of Engagement.' That is the only sense you then get out of that and I think that is a very important point that came out of yesterday's discussions.

Malcolm Dando: I think what we are trying to emphasise is that there is a great deal of information surrounding the sinking of the Belgrano which is not yet in the public domain and one of the functions of this Enquiry is to try at least to understand clearly what we don't know.

Paul Rogers

What I would like to do is to reiterate briefly the sequence of events leading up to the sinking of the Belgrano and to look at two events in particular which seem to me to provide really remarkably hard evidence that military escalation was what was actually happening. Despite the British Government's claim that in the first two days of May it was pursuing a policy of minimum force in pursuit of a diplomatic settlement, it was actually pursuing a policy of maximum force in pursuit of a military settlement.

To give a little bit of background first: when the first elements of the Task Force were despatched to the South Atlantic after the Argentinian invasion at the beginning of April, the size of the force sent built up over about three weeks. And it came to have two basic components, a Carrier Battle Group, two aircraft carriers and a wide variety of supporting ships which provided the air and sea fire power of the full Task Force, followed about a fortnight later by another group of ships called the Amphibious Task Group which contained all the troops, the Commandos and the Paras who were going to land on the Falklands when the air zone and the sea around the Falklands had been cleared of Argentine forces by the Carrier Battle Group. The Carrier Battle Group arrived in the area of the Falklands at the end of April. The Amphibious Task Group arrived about the middle of May, so there was basically about a 17 or 18 day period when the Carrier Battle Group was within range of the Islands and in a position to try and gain air superiority over the Argentinian airforces, both from the mainland and those actually on the Islands. I think this is a necessary background.

The Haig mission of course ended on the 30th April, to be followed by the development of peace initiatives by the Peruvians and the continuation, indeed the upgrading of peace initiatives by the United Nations. We know that the order to sink the aircraft carrier was given on the 30th April and we know that the Belgrano was tracked from, certainly visually by the 1st May and was finally sunk on the evening of the 2nd May.

Before I look at that military sequence I would just like to add one thing in relation to what Diana has said about the possible role of Lord Hugh Thomas. Before the 1983 election for a variety of reasons the sinking of the Belgrano rather briefly became an area of controversy, as a result of which a couple of newspapers, one the Daily Mirror, did a lot of background work into the circumstances surrounding the Peruvian Peace Plan and the sinking of the Belgrano. And among other things they put out feelers to freelance journalists in Latin America to follow up various leads. One particular journalist who acts as a stringer for a number of newspapers is a person called Mike Reed who is normally resident in Lima. He, among other things, interviewed the Peruvian Prime Minister at the time of the Falklands war, Manuel Ulloa. About three years ago I was shown the full telex that Reed sent to the Daily Mirror of the interview and of other interviews he conducted. And among other things that Manuel Ulloa told him was that the Peruvians were in contact with London in relation to their peace initiative both before and after the sinking of the Belgrano, and one of the contacts was a Mr Thomas. That was actually in the telex sent to the Daily Mirror. Nobody I think at the time realised the significance and from memory, as I say I saw this three years ago, it said specifically that this Mr Thomas was involved before as well as after the sinking of the Belgrano. That however is a digression, but I think it is an important one in relation to what Diana was saying a few minutes ago.

Let me go on to describe the circumstances of that first weekend in May. You may possibly recall that about 36 hours before the Belgrano was actually torpedoed, the Carrier Battle Group of the Task Force conducted a number of raids on Stanley, particularly the airbase and Argentine positions around Port Stanley and also on Goose Green. The almost universal interpretation of these raids as given to the British media by the Minister of Defence was that these raids were very much a part of the policy of minimum force. They were concerned with one specific function only and that was cutting the runway of the Stanley airbase to prevent Argentina resupplying its forces on the Falklands by air. In other words to combine an air blockade with the existing sea blockade which was being conducted by our nuclear powered submarines including H.M.S. Conqueror. That was the impression given and the impression believed. The minimum force idea was what our forces were about.

Inevitably after a major conflict like the Falklands war, there are many detailed technical analyses by defence analysts of the actual sequences of events. And in the case of that particular weekend a great deal has come out in the military literature as to what actually happened, and you actually find a very different pattern of events from that indicated to us. Specifically, the first stage of the raid on Stanley, and there were three stages, was a flight from Ascension Island by a Vulcan bomber and the dropping of one

particular pattern of bombs across the airstrip. There were in fact
21 bombs dropped in a single stick. The first three and the last
three of these were not anti-runway high explosive bombs but
cluster bombs. About three hours or so after the Vulcan dropped
its bombs, a very large raid was mounted by all the available strike
aircraft from H.M.S. Invincible and H.M.S. Hermes, Harrier and
Sea-Harrier aircraft. Some of the aircraft maintained a combat air
patrol over the area, the rest moved in to attack both Stanley and
Goose Green. The munitions used were high explosive bombs,
toss-bombed from outside the immediate area and fused for
air-burst not ground-burst, fused to burst over the runway and the
airfield and the facilities in a fragmentation pattern. The other
munition used was the BL755 cluster bomb. Now a cluster bomb
is not in fact a bomb at all, it is basically a container which in the
case of this particular weapon carries 147 bomblets, each of which
explodes and produces a kind of grenade effect, producing about
2,000 fragments. The bomblets explode over an area of about 1
1/2 acres showering the whole area in very high velocity fragments.
They have a devastating effect against what the technical literature
euphemistically calls 'soft targets', particularly people. These
bombs were used extensively in this raid and the raid on Goose
Green which of course was not even part of the resupply route
from the mainland. It did not have a runway suitable to take the
Hercules transports. In fact the assessment of the damage done
to the Stanley runway after these two raids, the Vulcan and the
Harrier raids, was that just one bomb from the Vulcan had hit the
runway. No other munitions had even hit the runway itself.

About four hours after the Harrier raids, we're now round about
lunchtime on the 1st May, three ships of the Task Force were
detached from the main part of the Task Force and moved in to
conduct a naval gunnery bombardment against the Stanley facility;
the ships were I believe the Glamorgan, Arrow and Alacrity. The
sustained barrage that these ships conducted with their 4.5 inch
radar-controlled guns was designed to continue the pattern of
destruction on the Stanley base. The shells were fused for air-burst
not ground-burst, again the aim being to produce a shrapnel cloud
over the actual base itself presumably while the repair teams were
trying to repair the damage which had been caused by the earlier
attacks in the day.

So what you have stated was an attack to cut the runway. What
you have in practice was a massive anti-personnel raid which in
fact caused considerable casualties. There were 56 Argentinians
killed or injured, 19 killed and 37 injured in that particular raid
alone. This tends to suggest that the military imperative was
uppermost even 36 hours or so before the Belgrano itself was sunk.

The second point I'd like to cover in relation to this sequence of events concerns the Belgrano itself and curiously I'm not actually concerned with the events leading up to the sinking. It is in some ways strange that when one is trying to look back and analyse the motives behind events, it sometimes turns out that you get the firmest indication not from the actual events themselves, but either from the preceding sequence or the after sequence and that is so in this particular case. Let me remind you that the view from the U.K. Government is that there was no knowledge of the Peruvian Peace Initiative or as they themselves called it the Peruvian/American Peace Initiative, there was no knowledge of that initiative until two hours or more after the Belgrano had actually been sunk. Only then did a message come from Washington, followed in the very early hours of Monday morning May 3rd by message from Lima and the Government line all along has been that nothing was known about the Peruvian Peace Plan before those messages were received. Tam Dalyell I think probably yesterday will have indicated otherwise and there's the possibility of the relationship with Lord Hugh Thomas, which again is still somewhat circumstantial.

What I want to focus on is the military actions conducted after the Belgrano was sunk. When Conqueror reported to Northwood that it had torpedoed the Belgrano late on the evening of the 2nd May, it received from London a signal instructing it to continue its anti-shipping patrol and to attack any Argentine surface ships inside or outside the Exclusion Zone. And this was a signal which had been sent to all the ships of the Task Force. The key point is that that signal was not countermanded from London even when the details of the Peruvian Peace Plan were known. It even goes further than this and I'll have to go into just a slight bit of detail here. When the torpedoes struck the Belgrano, in fact when the first of the two torpedoes struck the Belgrano, it destroyed all the major lighting circuits in the ship. The cruiser sank within about an hour and was in almost total darkness. The ship was accompanied by two destroyers. They tried to find the submarine, the Conqueror, and in fact there was even some depth charging in the area in which the Conqueror was presumed to be. In the rising seas and the onset of darkness the destroyers could not tell what had happened to the Belgrano because that had lost all radio communication and virtually all lights as well. One of the destroyers, as far as one can tell maybe two to three miles distance from the point where the Belgrano was torpedoed, observed lights in the water and believed that the cruiser was still afloat, but crippled and in radio silence. In fact the cruiser sank within an hour and the lights were the lights from some of the floats and the rafts on which some of the crew were. The destroyer signalled to base that the Belgrano was crippled but not sunk and then contact was lost with the rafts as nightfall and higher seas ensued. In fact if you look at the headline of the Sun newspaper, 'Gotcha! Our lads sink gunboat and hole cruiser', because the point is that the signal from the destroyer to the Argentinian headquarters was intercepted by British forces and was communicated to London. So on the night of the 2nd and 3rd May when we had receipt of the Peruvian Peace Plan in the Foreign Office, the Government, the Ministry of Defence at least, was actually under the impression that the Belgrano had not sunk, it had been crippled and the Sun obviously got hold of that story in the early hours of the morning.

What then happened was that on the 3rd May the Conqueror returned to the datum, that is the point where the Belgrano had been torpedoed, in order to have another go at the crippled cruiser and any of the destroyers lying in the vicinity. This was at least 12 hours after the British Government had received details of the Peruvian Peace Plan. There was nothing to be found when the Conqueror edged near to the datum, there were no sounds coming from any ship engines, nothing could be detected on the sonar in relation to any ship in the area. By that time rescue ships had not yet arrived in the area. There would have been the survivors on the rafts but the Conqueror certainly wasn't going to get too close because of risk of any action against it from any destroyers that might have been in the vicinity. So the Conqueror withdrew, not having found any ships and not having found a crippled cruiser. But the point is it went back to the site 12 hours after we knew about the Peruvian Peace Plan. There was no rescinding of the order to sink Argentine shipping outside the Exclusion Zone even when we knew of the new peace initiative.

On the 4th May, another 24 hours later, the Conqueror returned to the site of the sinking, observed a hospital ship and a destroyer searching for survivors and withdrew under orders from London. By the 4th May the Peruvian Peace Plan had been completely turned down by the Argentinians in the wake of the Belgrano sinking and no further immediate action was taken against Argentine shipping. I mention that last sequence because this particular information was raised during the Foreign Affairs Committee proceedings and in fact Mr Heseltine on one occasion was actually asked about this sequence of events and he glossed over it by saying that when the Conqueror returned to the site on the 4th May it was given orders not to sink any ships. He ignored the fact that we had learned from other sources that the Conqueror had returned on the 3rd May.

So in summary what I'm trying to say is to add two elements to what is already fairly widely known. One is that on the 1st May the military action taken against the Argentinian positions on the Falklands was not consistent with the policy of cutting the runway to maintain the air blockade as part of a policy of minimum force. The second point, and personally I think this is probably one of the most significant aspects of the whole sequence of events, is what happened after the cruiser was sunk. The fact that no attempt was made to ease off the forces opposing the Argentine navy even when it was know that a brand new peace plan was in the offing, the Peruvian/American Peace Plan.

Malcolm Dando: Just to be clear about this, on the evidence that we have available they knew about the Peruvian Peace Plan. It may well be that they knew a long time before.

Paul Rogers: That's right.

Malcolm Dando: On their own evidence.

Paul Rogers: On the Government's own evidence there was knowledge of the Peruvian Plan two hours after the Belgrano was attacked, two and a half hours.

Diana Gould: We did invite Lord Hugh Thomas to come to our Enquiry. He declined, and there is something very significant in that there were newspaper reports of his alleged involvement in all this. He has never ever issued any denial, he's never said anything, he's just keeping dead silence. You can draw your own conclusions.

Richard Baker: Could we just talk about the bombing of the runway? Was Paul Rogers saying that the only bombs dropped, anti-personnel, were not going to damage the runway?

Paul Rogers: No, the bombs dropped by the Vulcan in the night included both anti-personnel and anti-runway bombs, and one of those bombs was the only one in the whole operation which actually hit the runway. As far as we can tell, the bombs dropped by the Sea-Harriers were of three kinds, the cluster bombs which could not harm the runway itself but could wreak havoc on the surrounding area, air-burst high explosive bombs which again produce the shrapnel effect, and there were in fact delayed-action high explosive bombs dropped as well which would explode in later hours. As far as the information suggests, and I've checked the technical literature very specifically, there was no direct attempt to actually break open the runway in the Sea-Harrier raid.

Richard Baker: But if the runway was damaged directly or indirectly isn't it arguable that anti-personnel bombs would be dropped to prevent it being repaired?

Paul Rogers: Delayed-action bombs certainly, the anti-personnel bombs BL755 cluster bomb does not have a delayed-action component in it. So certainly, I should perhaps make this point,

I'm not saying that the Vulcan raid was not intended to break the runway. The Vulcan raid had that as part of its function. What I'm saying is that apart from breaking the runway the raids themselves were far wider than that and they were specifically anti-personnel at the time. They were not concerned just to destroy the runway.

Richard Baker: But wouldn't it be justifiable to attack the people who were repairing or might be available to repair the runway? Wouldn't there be justification for anti-personnel bombs for that reason?

Paul Rogers: Oh absolutely, I mean this is the military justification. I suppose what I'm arguing is that from a military point of view, you were concerned with maximizing the impact of the weapons at your disposal. But what this meant in the political sense was a much greater escalation of the conflict than was indicated by the British Government at the time. This was within the political context of minimum force when there were peace negotiations still in progress.

Richard Baker: What is the normal military procedure if you want to damage a runway... the rules and the doctrine of the RAF?

Paul Rogers: It's changed a lot in recent years. You now have munitions available which were not available to the Royal Air Force at the time.

Richard Baker: What was the doctrine at the time?

Paul Rogers: The doctrine at the time would have been more or less as it was followed, except that the raids on Stanley and Goose Green were far wider than just breaking the runway. The point about the raids was that Stanley didn't just contain the runway and the planes, it contained almost all the Argentine army concentrations near Port Stanley. Goose Green itself was one of the subsidiary army and airforce bases which had local planes rather than transport planes from the mainland. The attack on the Saturday was against the runway, the airbase, the army facilities and the facilities of Goose Green. It went far wider than the military basis of actually breaking the runway and keeping it broken.

John Ferguson: I think, if I can just come in for a moment, what surprised me about what Paul Rogers said was that if this was a succession of anti-personnel attacks in fact, that the casualties were so low.

Paul Rogers: I think the point here is that the Argentinians were relatively well dug-in and in addition these were the casualties as given by Argentina. Whether they relate to the full casualties we don't know. What they said, about three days later, was 56 killed and injured. There are certain suspicions that the figure was much higher than that.

Richard Baker: Another question I want to make, that during the war, I know it's hard to believe, about Lord Hugh Thomas: is this a suggestion that he was acting, I don't know anything about Lord Hugh Thomas, was he acting on behalf of the Government? What office did he hold?

Paul Rogers: Lord Thomas is a well known contemporary historian, an expert principally on Spanish and Latin American affairs. He wrote what is undoubtedly the standard work on the Spanish Civil War and he wrote probably the standard work on Cuba. He has for the last, I think it must be going on for 10 years, been a personal policy adviser for the present Prime Minister Mrs Thatcher, both I think before she came to office and while she's been in office. In other words, you have at the level of individual ministers and indeed Prime Minister, you often have unofficial advisers. Sometimes they hold appointments, sometimes they're unofficial advisers. Lord Thomas occupied that position. He particularly was one of the very small group of independent foreign policy advisers and his area covered Latin America. He knew many people in the Peruvian Government personally.

Malcolm Dando: Paul, one technical matter I think we ought to cover, can you tell us a little bit about British nuclear weapons and the conflict in the Falklands? Specifically, what do we know about the tactical nuclear weapons which were taken or not taken down on our ships and secondly, what do we know about any involvement of British strategic nuclear weapons?

Paul Rogers: It is a fairly complicated matter. Could I just mention two things initially. The kinds of nuclear weapons which could conceivably have been deployed in the South Atlantic are basically three sorts. There is the Polaris strategic nuclear missile on Polaris submarines and there are two kinds of Naval tactical nuclear weapons. One is a free-fall nuclear bomb which can be delivered by Sea-Harrier jump-jets operating off Hermes or Invincible; the other is an anti-submarine nuclear depth bomb which can be delivered by helicopters against submarines. And in fact all the frigates and destroyers in the Royal Navy that can embark an anti-submarine helicopter, that's about 50 ships, can in fact deploy these tactical anti-submarine nuclear depth charges. Those are the three classes of weapon which are available and would have been available at the time for use in the South Atlantic.

It is certainly true, and this is known from good sources, that a number of ships which went as part of the Carrier Battle Group towards the Falklands at the beginning of April 1982 carried tactical nuclear weapons. Ships which had either already been on patrol as part of a NATO exercise in the Mediterranean and indeed to my knowledge at least one ship which actually left

Britain. The commander of one particular frigate said that he was only prepared to go into what might be a war zone if he was carrying a full complement of weapons including nuclear depth bombs. And in fact John Nott in his statement the day the Task Force sailed, actually made it clear for those who were aware of the technicalities, he used the phrase the ships would be equipped with 'their full range of weapons'. Very few people realised at the time exactly what that phrase means. The understanding that I have is that there was a considerable controversy within Whitehall, particularly within the Ministry of Defence, as to whether it was wise to even send ships equipped with tactical nuclear weapons into this kind of potential conflict with a non-nuclear power. And such was the opposition within certain circles within the Ministry of Defence, that some and possibly all of the tactical nuclear weapons were taken off the Carrier Battle Group ships at or near Ascension Island. I don't know whether all of them were removed, but certainly some. And I know as much as to say that they were transferred to a Royal Fleet Auxiliary, H.M.S. Regent, which was then kept out of the Falklands war zone because it had these tactical nuclear weapons on board. Although it may well have gone down to the South Atlantic quite close to the Falklands with them on board in its munitions armoury, but it was kept at least near South Georgia for the major duration of the conflict. It is possible that some of the ships in the war zone still had their nuclear weapons on board but there is conflicting evidence on this. Certainly they headed south and certainly at least one ship left Britain having taken on board tactical nuclear weapons.

The other side of the whole business concerns strategic nuclear weapons, which in my view is far more significant, and this relates to information which was given to Mr Dalyell in the spring of 1983. He was told by a senior and experienced Conservative backbencher with a longstanding interest in defence matters that the Task Force had been backed up by a Polaris missile submarine and that the Government had the option of being able to threaten a nuclear strike on Argentina using Polaris missiles if things went grieviously wrong for the Task Force. This information in fact was published in a couple of papers, the Guardian paid tiny service to it, Tribune splashed it I think at the time. No further information on this was available except from this one source, who of course refused to be named and would deny knowledge of it if Tam named him.

During the development of the Belgrano controversy in the summer of 1984 with the arrest of Clive Ponting, in fact round about that time, the New Statesman gained independent evidence supporting this story and to my knowledge that has come also in the last two years from two other sources associated with the Ministry of Defence and indeed one source to Tam Dalyell, an officer from within the Polaris fleet.

Putting all together the different aspects of the story we have the following. Right at the start of the conflict when the Task Force was actually starting to get under way, contingency plans were drawn up as to what losses might be suffered. And one of the options which was expressed as being available was to deploy some sort of nuclear capability. But this, at least at the strategic level of a Polaris submarine was actually not considered appropriate at the time.

On the 4th May, two days after the Belgrano was sunk, H.M.S. Sheffield was hit by an Exocet missile and within a few hours reduced to a smouldering wreck, 20 or so people dying and many others being injured. H.M.S. Sheffield was the lead ship of a Type 42 Class and it was a Class dedicated to air defence. It was one of the most modern ships in the Navy, the Type 42 Class was still being built, in fact we're still just completing the last of them now, and it was a tremendous shock to the Navy. It was a shock to Britain, but it was a much greater shock at a technical level to the Royal Navy because this ship was effectively destroyed by one Exocet missile and Argentina had several more of them and the means to deliver them. I might say that one or two defence analysts had predicted, even before the conflict developed, that this was the one weak point in the Navy's armoury, and this actually proved to be the case.

As far as is known, and this comes from several sources, mainly leaks to Mr Dalyell, once the Sheffield had been sunk it was recognised that there was a real, in fact a very high risk, that the Argentine naval aviation service would try to strike with its remaining Exocets at any of three targets; one of the two aircraft carriers Invincible or Hermes, or the troop ship Canberra. And the logistic fact of the matter was quite clearly that if any one of those ships had been crippled or sunk the retaking of the Falkland Islands could not have been conducted before the onset of the South Atlantic winter. In other words the Task Force would have had to withdraw and almost without question Mrs Thatcher would have fallen from office in the consequences of that disaster.

It was at that time that the decision apparently was taken to deploy a Polaris submarine within range of Argentina. The range of the Polaris missiles is such that the submarine was located some hundreds of miles south-west of Ascension Island, just into the South Atlantic, south of the equator. It did not have to go anywhere near the Falkland Islands themselves. It would have been in fact 3,000 miles north of the Falkland Islands. That was within the missile range of Argentina, particularly the Argentine military complex of Cordoba in Northern Argentina and this, Tam was told, was the specified target. He has never claimed and I have not been able to get further information on this, that there was any decision to carry out that threat if it ever had to be made, but the means to make it was actually set up, so that if the Task Force was faced with withdrawal, there was this hold at least to be used in private, over the Argentine government. That is effectively all the information that is known from the leaks but in fact other information has become known from a quite different source which, though circumstantial, is worth mentioning albeit briefly.

At the time of the Falklands war Britain had 11 nuclear-powered hunter-killer submarines available. One of them was Conqueror. And according to the British Government, five of those submarines were deployed in the Falklands area to act as forward protection to the Task Force ships, forming a barrier between the Argentine coast and the area of Task Force operations. Those boats, the submarines, were particularly concerned with preventing attacks by Argentine surface craft, including the Belgrano, and with trying to counter the fear of the quiet Argentine diesel submarines of which there were two very modern West German boats in service with the Argentine navy. So we are told that there were five submarines in service in that area. There were 11 available of which perhaps seven were actually ready. Others would have been refitting and undergoing long repairs. So if five submarines were down there, seven were available.

What is now known is that two submarines were guarding the Polaris boat in the mid-Atlantic and this comes from an entirely different leak. And what is interesting is that we have firm direct evidence of the pattern of the submarine operations in the war zone itself, and it turns out that in fact there were never five submarines down there. Only right at the end of the war were there even four, and for the key period of the war right up until just before the landings at San Carlos there were only three of these submarines protecting the entire Task Force. In other words there were not enough to go round. There were not enough to get them from Britain down to the South Atlantic and from Britain to protect the Polaris submarine and continue normal protection of our Polaris submarine in the North Atlantic and to protect the Task Force fully. And in fact, of the three submarines which were present in the war zone for the key period of the war, one of them went into serious mechanical trouble, H.M.S. Splendid, and had to be withdrawn out of the immediate war zone. And Conqueror, for at least a week, operated on only half capacity because of a steam leak and shaft noise problems. So serious was the lack of submarine cover in the war zone itself that at one stage an attempt was made to airlift a crucial mechanical part to Splendid, a 15,000 mile round trip from Britain down, stopping at Ascension Island, involving multiple air-refuelling with the piece air-dropped to the submarine lying off South Georgia, semi-crippled. The air drop failed, as the parachute failed to open and the spare part was lost. And Splendid did not take any full part in the campaign and was withdrawn long before the end of the war.

Now this is circumstantial evidence but it demonstrates that the Government's claim that we had adequate forces protecting the Task Force, adequate nuclear hunter-killer submarines is actually false. We could not do both jobs at once, we couldn't protect the Polaris submarine in mid-Atlantic which had to be protected because apart from anything else there was very extensive Soviet activity in that area and we couldn't protect the Task Force as well, and the Polaris submarine took precedence as far as we can tell. It isn't conclusive evidence. it may well be that one of the reasons that log books have had a tendency to disappear is that they might tell us a lot more about this whole sequence of events. But the combination of the leaks from I think now five different sources and the circumstantial evidence in relation to hunter-killer submarines does lead to the conclusion that the option was made available to have a Polaris missile submarine with which to threaten Argentina if the need arose.

Richard Baker: Just a couple of brief questions about the tactical nuclear weapons, it may be well known but I don't know it. What would be the effect if any ship which carried tactical nuclear weapons were sunk? Where would the action of the fall-out or whatever be, how far would it extend?

Paul Rogers: Nuclear weapons are normally only finally armed and ready for firing very soon before they would actually be used, a matter of minutes or even seconds. In other words if a frigate which carried a helicopter which could take nuclear depth bombs, if the frigate loaded the helicopter with the bombs and the helicopter took off, those depth bombs would not be finally fully armed until they were about to be dropped. So in other words, on the ships themselves the weapons are in what is known as 'storage configuration' and the weapons themselves probably cannot explode as nuclear weapons. That may not have been true 30 years ago but things have got rather safer now. Nevertheless, the weapons themselves contain fissile material, plutonium in particular, and if they are destroyed in a fire or an explosion the plutonium can be distributed within the hull of the ship or indeed in the water round about. You would not get a nuclear explosion but you could get localised contamination.

Richard Baker: So there wouldn't be a major danger?

Paul Rogers: There wouldn't be a major danger, no. I mean, to give you an example, one of the worst nuclear accidents that has taken place so far was when an American B-52 crashed in Greenland and one of its H-bombs burnt up in the fire that ensued. In fact they had to decontaminate a section of the ice cap, removing 1 1/2 million gallons of snow and ice to permanent storage in the United States to allow the radioactive contamination to decay. So it would be localised rather than like the effects of a nuclear weapon.

Joan Hymans: We know that the Belgrano had turned back when it was hit but Mrs Thatcher insisted on saying it had to be sunk because it was a danger to our forces. how far was it actually from us, was it in fact a danger?

Paul Rogers: It was around about 200 to 240 miles from the Task Force unit. The map down there, which is actually based on a Ministry of Defence presentation to the Select Committee, showed fairly clearly that the Belgrano was to the southwest of the Exclusion Zone which itself was 200 mile radius from the Falklands. So as a minimum, the Belgrano at all times would have been about 200 miles from the Task Force, at the time it was sunk it was probably nearer 300 miles. What I think is perhaps important here is that if the Belgrano had become a threat to the Task Force by heading towards the Task Force, it would have had to enter the Exclusion Zone, and the orders already existed to the Conqueror's captain to sink it if it entered that zone and headed for the Task Force. In fact one of the officers on the Conqueror recorded in his diary that they found it rather frustrating that the Belgrano was carefully keeping away from the Exclusion Zone, not going in any way towards the area where it might be perceived as a threat. If it was to become a threat, the orders were there to sink it. I think that's possibly the most crucial point.

Joan Hymans: So it wasn't in fact a threat.

Paul Rogers: No.

Nick Kollerstrom: You argued about the return of the Conqueror on the 3rd May. Nott testified, and Lewin and Heseltine, about this to the Foreign Affairs Committee and they all give answers quite contradictory to what you've just said. For example, Nott said 'Oh I expect it (the Conqueror) returned in order to try and pick up survivors', is the one that I recall. Do you not feel that because these three government experts all gave this quite opposite interpretation to yours concerning the return on the 3rd May, that you may be in error? Or, if not, how is such make-believe possible on the part of these three government authorities, concerning the purpose of the return?

Paul Rogers: I think I can just answer that in two ways. Firstly, if my version is correct, then one wouldn't expect the Government spokesman to agree with it in public, because it knocks a hole right through the Government's case in relation to the Peruvian Peace Plan. All I can say is that the information which I have came from an officer on the Conqueror who said what in fact the Conqueror was doing and why it was going back there to have a go at the Belgrano which they believed was still afloat, and indeed at any of the escorts they could find.

Denis Ridgeway: Mr Eric Ogden, Director of the Falkland Island Association, yesterday indicated, if I understood him correctly, that the Belgrano loss of life was so high on account of inefficiency on the part of the Belgrano after the hit, with the implication that the loss of life was unnecessarily high for this reason. Now I don't know whether Mr Ogden is here this morning but if he would consider that's a fair interpretation of what he said, then I would like to ask Dr Rogers if he would like to comment on this view?

Paul Rogers: Well, let me just present another view. You'll find in the appendix to the Select Committee Report a reprint of probably the most detailed account of the behaviour of the Argentine forces during the Falklands war. It's written by Dr Robert Scheina who is a United States academic, in fact he is the official historian of the U.S. Coastguard Service and he is probably the leading expert on Latin American navies. And he gives a great deal of detail about the attack on the Belgrano and its consequences for the crew. One thing is clear, is that the Belgrano itself was not at 'Action Stations' since it was outside the Exclusion Zone and heading towards home waters; it was not expecting it to be attacked. It was not even using its sonar at the time. This again is recorded from crew on the Conqueror.

What actually happened when the Belgrano was attacked was that one of the torpedoes, and these were Mark 8, I think 800 pound warheads, very large torpedoes, very powerful ones, one of the torpedoes effectively broke the back of the cruiser and exploded amidships, in and under one of the mess decks and caused huge casualties within the first few seconds of the detonation. The Belgrano lost all steerage, lost all power, lost all power supplies and heeled over to a list of about 15 degrees within a matter of about a minute or so. So it was a ship in pitch darkness and it was a ship also which remember carried a crew of 1100, most of whom were young conscripts, because it was the main training ship of the Argentine Navy. They then evacuated in the 45 minutes remaining while the ship was still fully afloat, and something like 700 people got off. In fact, Scheina's view was that the casualities were remarkably low considering the conditions and considering the immediate effect of the torpedo strike. Now Scheina is not an Argentinian, he is a U.S. academic and he's an expert on Latin American naval affairs. He interviewed a number of the survivors of the Belgrano, including I think, the captain. That is his particular view.

Bill Hetherington: Paul Rogers suggested that the policy was one of maximum military force, as shown by the use of anti-personnel bombs at Port Stanley and Goose Green, and also by the attack on the Belgrano itself. That was my own view right from the 3rd April, right from the news that the Task Force was being sent. But one knows that many people now are saying, 'Well we never expected it to turn out like this, we thought it would be all over without any real fighting.' I wonder whether, in view of the way people are saying from hindsight how they thought it would turn out, what concrete evidence you may be able to use to show that right from the 3rd April we should accept that the Government's mood was maximum military force rather than solve the problem by diplomacy?

Paul Rogers: I think one has to define the term 'Government' very carefully and for my part I think there are probably three different components. You have the Navy itself, particularly senior officers and particularly I think Lord Lewin: there was the immediate entourage of the Prime Minister, Mrs Thatcher and Mr Parkinson, and there were people such as Mr Nott and Mr Pym. I can't give a hard and fast answer. My inclination is to think that as April progressed the armed forces, particularly the senior naval people, looked more and more at an early stage to a military solution. And I think probably that developed within the, if I might call it, the Prime Minister's component of the War Cabinet. We do know again that a signal was sent to submarines in the South Atlantic, on I think it was the 26th April, saying that the diplomatic posturing is over and a military solution is now anticipated. That was when the Government was still saying something different. So I think the point is, different people were saying and maybe even thinking different things. My own belief is that certainly by the end of April the military adjuncts of government, and the Prime Minister herself and her immediate close associates were concerned with a military solution primarily. And maybe other people within the War Cabinet, certainly within the Cabinet which was not at that time meeting at all, may have been concerned still with a diplomatic settlement.

What I think is very well worth bringing in at this stage is comment by Jim Prior in his memoirs recently, in which he says that if the Peruvian plan, or U.N. plan, or Haig plan had been agreed and a negotiated settlement ensued in early May, there would have been a wholesale revolt among the Conservative backbenchers with up to 60 members revolting and I think up to 30 refusing the Government Whip. Now bearing in mind that the Conservative majority at that time was only 35, then Prior is saying that his opinion is that the Government would have fallen if it had tried to go for a negotiated settlement. That I think is a very interesting thing and I'm surprised more people have not realised the importance of it, because that was not the impression in the country at the time.

Mary Georghiou: This derives from the fact that you're very dependent on leaked sources and leaks and I want to say, if you suspect that this has been a cover-up and the importance that had on the re-election of the Thatcher government, how do you protect yourself from deliberate disinformation and leaks which have been put about to discredit you?

Paul Rogers: I think what you always try to do is to use as many different sources as you can. I think the one advantage in the kind of work that I've been interested in, is dealing more with military matters. There is actually a wide range of information which has been published. The war has been gone over and over by analysts in Britain, in the United States, and incidentally for that matter in the Soviet Union. And a tremendous amount has actually come out in great detail about the conduct of the war and this is not disinformation in any sense. This is the sort of factual basis that has come in to the defence community's eye. So we are not dealing with classified information, this is all open source information provided you know where to look. Now I think disinformation is obviously a problem and there was clearly a degree of disinformation during the conduct of the Select Committee proceedings. We had one example of it recently in terms of the question of going back to look for survivors. All I can say is that you go for a number of different sources and you don't normally talk about what you know until you have enough evidence to convince yourself that it is as genuine as one can ever hope for.

Richard Baker: Is Mr Rogers saying that, with the exception of people like Mr Dalyell, most members of Parliament are not making use of information such as his and what other people have got, that members of Parliament are not using such information?

Paul Rogers: I think they are increasingly but I think the problem with this particular sequence of events is there is an incredible amount of detail and one has to be very au fait with a huge range of issues and frankly there are very few members of Parliament who have had the time to specialise in it. Apart from Tam Dalyell,

a couple of Labour members of the Foreign Affairs Select
Committee, particularly Ian Mikardo and Nigel Spearing, very few
other people have actually gone into the details. John Morris, the
Labour Shadow Attorney-General, would be another one.

I have now actually got the section of Scheina's paper:

'The first torpedo hit under the aft 5 inch gun director and the
second hit on the port side forward of number one turret. The
first hit was the death blow, it raised the ship up in the water,
tore the emergency generators from their foundations and sent
a heat wave through the ship. The combination of the heat and
the explosion itself accounted for most of the casualties
suffered. Many sailors were resting in their quarters on the
orlop deck just aft of where the first torpedo hit. Immediately
forward of the blow sailors were crowded into the canteen to
buy personal items. Most of the people in these areas were
killed and they comprised 95% of those lost.'

Bill Hawthorn: This really arises out of yesterday's discussion of
the illegality or legality of the sinking and I would like you if you
would to clarify exactly the signals of statements made by the
British Government on Exclusion Zones and any amendments to
that before the sinking took place. Because as I understand it,
having declared an Exclusion Zone in which ships can be sunk, the
inference and the implication is that outside that Zone ships would
not be sunk and I would think that was the Argentinian
understanding of the situation. And I would think that is a fairly
solemn guarantee of the British Government and led the
Argentines to believe that as long as they stayed outside they
would not be sunk?

Then there was reference to a warning, and I'm not quite sure
of the wording of the warning, and presumably the warning was
public. But did that warning in effect amend the statement we
made about the Exclusion Zone, and if so did the Argentines
realise because of the warning that they were at risk outside?
Because I would point out yesterday when Mr Ogden was here,
he seems to have, in a rather cavalier fashion, dismissed British
Government's statements that he thought didn't mean anything
and I think that's a very dangerous road to pursue, especially for
small nations today...

Paul Rogers: I haven't actually come prepared to look at those
particular questions. I'll try and give a more general answer but
Diana may be able to be more specific and this is going from
memory. We can perhaps come back to you later in the day. From
what I remember the declaration of the Exclusion Zone before the
Belgrano was sunk specified that Zone as being the area in which
warships were at risk. It said that it didn't rule out normal

self-defence action under Article 51 of the U.N. Charter and that's
as far as it went. A more detailed statement, effectively giving
Argentina warning of British Government determination to sink
any ship which could be conceived of as a threat, was I think made
on May 7th, 5 days after the Belgrano was sunk. But Diana, can
you be more accurate on that?

Diana Gould: Item 13 on the top of page 6. This is the
Government White Paper replying to the Foreign Affairs
Committee. The whole section's entitled, 'The Warnings to
Argentina' and Item 13 says,

'With the benefit of hindsight the Government accepts that
there was and is misunderstanding about the purpose of the
Exclusion Zones which were created around the Falkland
Islands in 1982. However the warnings were explicit on the
point that, irrespective of the creation of the Maritime
Exclusion Zone, the M.E.Z. (which is the 7th April) later the
Total Exclusion Zone, the T.E.Z. (which came into being on
the 30th April), Her Majesty's Government reserve fully its
position in respect of the exercise of its right of self-defence
under Article 51 of the United Nations Charter. There has also
been confusion about the relationship between Exclusion
Zones, public warnings issued by Her Majesty's Government
during the Conflict and the Rules of Engagement.'

Now Admiral Lewin was asked similar questions on a Panorama
programme in April 1984, a very illuminating programme. he
explained this business of our rights if there was an immediate
threat. In his evidence to the Foreign Affairs Committee he
prevaricates asking 'How immediate is immediate?' But his
explanation is this: we had created the Exclusion Zones, the
Maritime Zone was just ships and the Total Exclusion Zone
included aircraft, but that did not mean to say that we gave up our
right to self-defence following an *immediate* threat anywhere in
the Atlantic.

So the warning of April 23rd which was given was really to try
to point that fact up, that we are not giving up our right of
self-defence. The official warning which was put out on April 23rd
was this:

'In announcing the establishment of a Maritime Exclusion Zone
around the Falkland Islands, Her Majesty's Government made
it clear that this measure was without prejudice to the right of
the United Kingdom to take whatever additional measures may
be needed in the exercise of its right of self- defence under
Article 51 of the United Nations Charter. In this connection
Her Majesty's Government now wishes to make clear that any
approach on the part of the Argentine warships, including

submarines, naval auxiliaries, or military aircraft which could amount to a threat to interfere with the *mission*'

this is the key word-

'of the British forces in the South Atlantic will encounter an appropriate response. All Argentine aircraft, including civil aircraft engaged in surveillance of these British forces, will be regarded as hostile and are liable to be dealt with accordingly.' Now there is another interesting fact about the warning which came out and is one of the questions which the Minority Report is asking, the Labour members were asking. Why was that warning not put into knowledge of Parliament quickly? In actual fact it was not deposited in the library, members of Parliament knew nothing of that warning for a further 11 days which if you add on to the 23rd April, I think you'll find that takes you after the sinking of the Belgrano. But it merely at the time was stating that we had created these Zones but of course if there's an immediate threat anywhere we will respond. And this is why yesterday when I was speaking, I asked the question that if this was their final justification, the Government's final justification for the sinking of the Belgrano, this warning of April 23rd — then what was the charade that took place on April 30th, the last time the Mandarins Committee was there to advise the Government, when in deciding whether we would sink the aircraft carrier or not, we went through the whole question of the range of its weapons, which was 400 miles because they were aircraft. They went through all that on the 30th to justify the sinking of the carrier. They could have justified it on this warning of April 23rd if that is valid for justifying the sinking of the Belgrano.

Going back again to that business on April 30th in the Foreign Affairs Committee Report you will see the question to Lord Lewin, when they decided on April 30th to sink the aircraft carrier, did the decision to sink the carrier include the sinking of her escorts? And Lord Lewin said, "Oh no, because you see the escorts only had Exocet, a range of 40 miles. They would not be a threat until they came within 40 miles." And two days later we sunk the Belgrano which had a gun range, and no Exocet, a gun range of 13 miles. This is really the crux of the whole matter.

WAR DIARY

2 April	Argentina invades Falklands.
5 April	Carrier Battle Group leaves Portsmouth
9 April	Most of the Amphibious Task Group sails.
19 April	Three SSN, *Spartan, Conqueror* and *Splendid*, all in the Falklands area.
29 April	Carrier Battle Group arrives off Falklands.
1-2 May	Britain escalates war — bombs and bombards Stanley air base and sinks *Belgrano*. Argentina retaliates with raids on CBG ships.
4 May	*Sheffield* sunk. Polaris submarine and escorting SSN deployed SW of Ascension Island soon afterwards.
To 7 May	Amphibious Task Group assembling at Ascension.
7 May	ATG leaves Ascension. *Conqueror* has steam leak and shaft problems. *Splendid* has serious generator problem.
8 May	*Splendid* withdraws to South Georgia. Only two SSN operational and *Conquerer* still with mechanical problems.
9 May	*Conqueror's* problem worse — produces excess noise above 15 knots (only half maximum speed).
10 May	Attempt to air-drop essential equipment to *Splendid* fails.
12 May	*Splendid* still near South Georgia.
17 May	*Valiant* finally arrives — still only three SSN fully operational.
18-19 May	ATG and CBG ships rendezvous, crucial cross-decking operation undertaken.
21-23 May	San Carlos landings commence, *Antelope* and *Ardent* lost.
25 May	Worst day of war for UK — *Coventry* and *Atlantic Conveyor* lost.
27 May	*Splendid* routed home early.
30 May	*Courageous* arrives — four SSN finally fully operational in war zone.
7 June	*Spartan* routed home.
14 June	war ends.

VI

The Costs of the War

Paul Rogers, Diana Gould, Wade Tidbury

Paul Rogers

In addition to what has been said in the prologue, I'd like to give a little background as to how recent and present costs are being incurred. I think there are several points to be made. After the war was fought and for the next two to three years, substantial forces were maintained in the Falklands area. The total garrison 18 months after the war was of about 7,000 troops, about 3,000 to 4,000 army and very substantial airforce and naval contingents. Two years after the war the South Atlantic Peace Patrol, as the Royal Navy termed it, involved five destroyers or frigates at any one time on patrol in and around the Falklands area. Over the last two years a large converted merchant ship, converted into a helicopter carrier, has also been stationed down in the Falklands. Bearing in mind the distance, the pattern has been that a ship would undergo a five-month deployment, a month in transit down, three months on deployment, and then a month back. Ships would also need all kinds of repairs, fuelling up, preparations and the rest, short-term refits and the like and because of the transit time as well, for every ship actually on patrol you needed roughly two and a half ships available, to allow for transit, fuelling up and all the rest. And that I think is a very conservative estimate.

So in fact over the period after the war and certainly for the first two to three years, we had five ships permanently down there, which means we were committing at least 12 of the destroyers and frigates of the Royal Navy. At the time there were about 53 escorts in Royal Naval service overall, of which at any one time about three quarters are available, in other words they're not on long-term, one-year refits. So consequently at least a quarter and getting on for a third of the Royal Navy's entire escort fleet was for over two years concerned with the defence of the Falkland Islands.

That has now dropped off considerably, bearing in mind that you have a civilian government in Argentina, the level of potential conflict has dropped, but even now, four years after the war, there is a patrol of two destroyers and frigates at any one time. At least five ships set aside from the total Royal Naval availability of about

40 ships. So even now about one eighth of the Royal Navy's surface capability is concerned with protecting the Falkland Islands.

Another aspect of the problem is that the Falkland Islands, covering an area larger than Wales, are very difficult to actually patrol and you have extensive use of helicopters as the main means of getting around. You have the very expensive Mount Pleasant facility, £400 million or so worth of airfield, barracks and the rest, you have a number of outlying areas and you have a number of radar facilities. So if you are trying to have an air bridge bringing in urgent supplies and troops, carriers and Phantoms for air protection, and a range of different helicopter types for routine resupply of the facilities around the Falklands, you have to have a very large backup force to keep them in the air. For example, the Chinook, the large R.A.F. helicopter has a basic, absolutely basic servicing crew of about 25 skilled personnel. So if you have say two or three of those aircraft you have that team there permanently. And that is true for any aircraft type. And then you have the backup to those personnel. Certainly two years ago, the R.A.F. alone had over 800 people on the Falkland Islands and that will not recede to any great extent.

The point I'm making is that maintaining this kind of force so far from home is a long term expensive facility. You can cut down the size of your troops to maybe one battalion, about 1,000 men, maybe even slightly less, but all the backup, the technical backup for the Navy and the Airforce has to stay permanently. And the indications are that at a minimum the permanent cost of maintaining Fortress Falklands will be about £250 million a year, on the Goverment's own estimates, indefinitely until a settlement is actually reached. The problem is that geo-political facts lie against Britain in maintaining Fortress Falklands. It is very close to Argentina and unless there is a firm peace treaty the minimum force that has to be maintained now is actually substantial. I estimate that at any time, no matter how much the garrison is cut down, there is going to be a minimum of 3,000 personnel based on the Falklands indefinitely until a settlement is reached.

Diana Gould

Simply quoting the figures given for the dead, missing and wounded in the Falklands War gives no inkling of the continuing tragedy of the lives of those affected. The families of the dead have had to learn to live without the husband, father or son who was killed 8,000 miles from home. The maimed have had to try to make new lives, perhaps without a limb, or with tragically disfiguring injuries from terrible burns. Little is heard of those who suffered psychologically, but some men have literally had to learn to live again.

The bereaved families of the British war victims have been able to visit the far-away graves. But for the relatives of the Argentine dead, even that is denied them. The recent burial of a young Argentinian pilot discovered in the wreckage of his plane has highlighted this situation. His father and sister were allowed to attend the funeral. However, in order to do so they had to travel to this country and then to the Island, 16,000 miles, when the distance from the South American coast is about 400 miles. Mr Gimenez would have liked his son to have been buried in his home town, but Argentina refused to repatriate the bodies of the war dead since according to them they are buried on Argentine territory i.e. the Malvinas.

Whether it may now prove possible for other relatives to visit the Argentinian burial ground remains to be seen, but previous attempts have foundered over Argentina's refusal to accept conditions and wording which it says imply recognition of British rule. In a correspondence I have had with an Argentine member of Rotary International, he has asked me if the Belgrano Action Group could ask the British Red Cross International to contact its namesake in Argentina so that pressure could be brought to alter that wording and make it acceptable.

I had hoped to get some of the relatives to speak today, but the ones I approached found it too painful to do so. However I would like to read to you the letter that came to me from this Argentinian Rotarian, that was written to him by the mother of a young British sailor killed on the Coventry.

She wrote in reply to a letter from him:

'Dear Sir
Thank you for your letter, received today via Oxford Rotary Club. Yes, I went to the Islands to pay tribute to the memorials, especially HMS Coventry Cross on Pebble Island and to the sea grave of HMS Coventry on which my son Ian aged 22 years died. His loss was great to us — too much for my husband — who became ill and died on January 29th 1985 aged 53 years. Ian was our only son, but I would like you to understand we have never blamed the ordinary Argentine people for our sad loss — for you too know the pain of losing loved ones. I blame only the politicians, and I wish they had talked together longer and not brought our two countries into conflict. It should not have happened.

I wanted to visit the Argentine Cemetery to say a prayer for all those young boys who died and for their sorrowing parents and other relations who must still feel such pain and suffering for the loss of all their young sons, as we do still ours. I hope it will be some comfort to you all to know the Argentine Cemetery is in a very quiet and peaceful location and the graves are well cared for, but I felt very sad that many were unnamed and only had the inscription "An Argentine soldier — known only to God". Many of those boys were so young — even younger than my own son! I remember reading somewhere that "Grief has no nationality", and this is indeed true for we all suffer the same heartache.

To all those who lost loved ones in the South Atlantic Conflict, I pray you find enough strength to bear the loss and may you find peace in your hearts soon'

After the war the bereaved found a lack of humanity, confusion and poor organisation in dealing with their needs and it took a campaign by a journalist, Jean Carr, in order to ensure that adequate compensation was eventually forthcoming for the relatives of the dead and for the medically discharged. She has chronicled this in a book, 'Another Story, Women and the Falklands War' and her feelings are possibly summed up in this sentence:

'It is appalling that a system that could so rapidly mobilise a 28,000 strong Task Force was so incapable of dealing with the consequences of such a brief, bitter war'

On the fourth anniversary of the war, earlier this year, members of the Malvinas Veterans Group which represents 6,000 of the 8,5000 soldiers who served in the Islands, set up a protest camp in the Plaza of the Republic in Buenos Aires. The plight of some of them is distressing as the Veterans Benefits Bill (1984) had not been passed by the Argentine Government and so former servicemen had not been given the tests they needed to determine what assistance they required to enable them to return to a normal life, and this is four years after the war.

The Islanders themselves have had to learn to cope with a different situation from pre 1982. Perhaps one way in which they have suffered is that their relatives have had to be brought to Britain when seriously ill and some have died here, thousands of miles from their own families. The opening of the new hospital next year will alleviate this difficulty but apparently the snag there is that the hospital is going to be extremely costly to operate.

Since the war young servicemen have died in accidents that have occurred whilst they have been helping to maintain Fortress Falklands, and such tragedies are bound to continue as long as we are keeping a large number of personnel on and around the Islands. The establishment from next February, of the Falkland Islands Interim Conservation and Management Zone (FICZ) of

150 miles and the formal assertion of the Government's right to a fisheries limit of 200 miles around the Islands, as announced at the end of October may possibly lead to patrols in hazardous weather and therefore to more casualties.

I wonder if the Islanders realise the awesome responsibility that has been thrust upon them by making their 'wishes' of paramount importance? When they hear of the vast sums that this country can ill afford, being spent on the Falklands; when they see pictures of the men terribly maimed, their lives shattered; when they think of the bereaved mothers and wives and fatherless children, do they not realise that this is the price to be paid by others, not themselves, for the veto that 'their wishes' effectively has put on any negotiations? I ask the question, do they count the cost?

I would now like to introduce to you Wade Tidbury who was in the Navy and was on the Alacrity in the South Atlantic during the Falklands Campaign.

Wade Tidbury
Well, on my thoughts on human costs I would first of all like to suggest that up to the point when the Belgrano was sunk the mood within the Alacrity had been that a massive naval presence plus the diplomatic effort would be successful and the Argentine would come to some agreement over the Islands with the British diplomats involved. After the Belgrano I can honestly say that everyone seemed to feel that the fighting had begun and all diplomatic negotiations, along with the Belgrano, had been sunk. From this we can assume then that the human costs of lives and suffering began with the loss of 368 lives. I'd like to stress at this point that the first loss of lives were at the encampments around Stanley airport which Paul Rogers covered quite extensively in the last session. The deaths, injuries and suffering from this sort of attack can only be imagined on one's worst nightmares.

But of the Belgrano, Eric Ogden spoke quite flippantly of the normal seas in the area when the Belgrano was sunk and he suggested that more should have survived because there was incompetence within the Argentine navy. I would like to say that this is a rather callous line. Normal seas in the area at that time of year is a very heavy swell with the waters being at temperatures which would allow a survival time for someone of just a few minutes before exposure to the cold would kill them. To give you some idea of what the situation would have been like, I would like to refer to personal experiences on the Alacrity, one of which I can recall quite vividly on the 25th May with the air attack on the Atlantic Conveyor. The ship was hit within a minute of Action Stations being sounded and Alacrity was detailed to do the rescue work. I reached the upper deck when the Conveyor was just a few miles away, a huge column of smoke rose upwards from the stern as we steamed towards the ship, hose reels laid out on our forecastle, and it took about 15 minutes for us to reach the ship, a huge container ship which towered over us. The black hull of the ship dwarfed the Alacrity as we edged nearer and nearer. A relatively small hole could be seen in the side of the ship where the missile had entered. Explosions could be heard, loud thuds from within, we assumed they were explosions from bombs going off, we didn't know. As people rushed around on the upper deck I saw small figures, some incredibly in fire-fighting gear, re-enter the ship. I've recently learned that people were attempting to rescue their fellow shipmates whose tortured screams they could hear trapped below. Paint began to peel off the side of the Conveyor from the heat within and the flames began to work their way onto the upper deck. Helicopters buzzed around and the Alacrity attempted to push the Conveyor around so wind and smoke were less of a problem. This futile gesture failed and things began to ignite on the upper deck of the Conveyor. A large Chinook helicopter strapped to the deck of the Conveyor was engulfed in flames. Ladders were put down the side of the ship and the order was given for them to abandon ship, and the life rafts dropped into the water. As the scramble down the ladder turned to near panic I saw a man fall from the top, an arm or a leg just snatched in the ladder and you could hear it crack, he then fell on into the water. He didn't move, he was dead.

The side of the sip was hot and many had difficulty using the rope ladders, there was shouting and screaming, helicopters, smoke and general confusion as the Atlantic Conveyor's crew made the short journey to the Alacrity. Some were picked up by helicopters, some made it to the life rafts, some even managed to swim to our ship. As I looked down from the forecastle I noticed one man floundering yards from the life raft, the cold waters were slowing him down and I took a length of rope and weighted it and threw it towards him. His arms moved backwards and forwards as he looked upwards towards the Alacrity. I shouted at him to take the rope and he ignored me. I swore at him, shouting myself hoarse, to take the rope, and someone grasped my shoulder, "He's dead, leave him." At that time I swore and screamed at the sky, not at the Argentines and not at anyone. The pointless waste and the disgusting, pointless waste of life through war filled me with tears. I felt I did not want any more of this war and the rest of the rescue work became a blur. We helped cold people out of wet clothes and shared food and hot drinks amongst us all. I grabbed a few cans of beer so I could calm myself before I returned to the radar screen and defence watches. It was to be almost three years before I could talk openly about that experience.

Help was at hand for the crew of the Conveyor. Within an hour people were being fed, clothed and treated. The horror of the Belgrano is that it seems our submarine the Conqueror did not leave the area immediately and the two escort ships were unable to return to the area to rescue people for almost 24 hours.

Overall, as with all wars, human costs are really incalculable. 1,060 were killed in the Falklands war, 770 British people were injured and an even higher number of Argentinians. The human costs and the suffering of British families is well documented in Jean Carr's book 'Another Story, Women and the Falklands War' in which I could quote many instances where the authorities wished to cover up the human suffering. I can quote from page 115 in the book:

'The expense of living with their injuries caused them even more domestic problems, Working wives took unpaid leave or gave up jobs to stay at home and nurse their men or spend the best part of the day with them in hospital. At home they were given the additional cost of providing extra meals, heating and special clothing. Soldiers whose burns were still being treated daily with medicated creams could only wear cotton fabrics next to their painfully sensitive skin. One wife had to borrow £300 from relatives to buy five complete sets of cotton clothes for her Welsh Guard husband, clothes that were changed and laundered twice a day as his skin creams soaked through. Men with amputations had to pay for taxis to get anywhere. They could no longer drive their cars or manage public transport while they were still getting used to their artificial limbs.

An army camp is very like a village, an enclosed community where neighbours know each others business and problems. Regimental officers must have been aware of the hardships some families faced but too few did anything. Numerous regiment's and Service charities exist to help families in these circumstances and the South Atlantic Fund gave £250,000 each to three principal Service charities specifically to help the injured. Four months after the return from the Falklands hardly any of that money had been spent on them because charity rules insist that payments can only be made to those who apply for help and can prove they need assistance. And we all know the parish pump atmosphere of the barrack room life, no one was going to belittle themselves by asking for charity or telling the Regiment's Paymaster they had money problems.'

Of course the most remembered example of the attempted cover-up of human suffering was at the Victory Parade in London.

The instructions given that no one in wheelchairs could be in the Parade, or no one could go in front of the crowd near the viewing balcony used by Mrs Thatcher. The other way the forces shunned the injured is by denying the fact that people can suffer mentally from the effects of war. Polly Tonybee's article interview with Surgeon Commander Morgan O'Connell in the Guardian of November '82 and again in the Guardian of November '83, Commander O'Connell was responsible for dealing with the 'transient situation disturbances' better known as shell-shock or battle-shock. In this interview it was revealed that 17 cases were reported by the Ministry of Defence of this disorder, yet 32 cases had been treated by Mr O'Connell. Many were denied treatment and many were shunned. A small quote from the article regarding a man whose illness, if that's what it can be called, was attributed to the war, Mr O'Connell said his illness was directly attributed to the war and when Polly Tonybee asked what was wrong with him he said, 'Reactive psychosis.'

'What is that?'

'Losing touch with reality and a conflict of ideology'

'What sort of conflict?'

'He had a strong feeling that the war should never have been allowed to happen. He could never manage to identify the Argentines sufficiently as enemies. He said he had no problems about the Russians but the Argentines were friends until a short time ago. He did see it was necessary for us to retake the Falklands but he thinks the invasion itself should have been prevented.'

Polly Tonybee asked why this view was regarded as a mental disease. He said,

'You have to remember what his job is. He's losing touch with reality. For as long as he is in this job this conflict is a problem to him. It handicaps him.'

He was regarded as mentally ill when others who were suffering from shell-shock and could not do any work whatsoever, pacing up and down for hours on end, unable to sleep suffering from nightmares, etc etc were denied help because they were told there was absolutely nothing wrong with them. Another quote from the situation in the land battle in the same interview:

'Junior officers made the most of Mr O'Connell's services — he was a psychiatrist with the fleet — consulting him about their men. One young officer whose men were sleeping in sheep-shearing huts came to him worried that they were all talking in their sleep and having nightmares. Commander O'Connell warned him that this was an early symptom of battle- shock and advised him to keep them busy, warm, dry and well- fed. He

ran a psychotherapy course for the survivors of the Ardent.
They needed to talk about their experiences. Some felt a lot of
anger, others a lot of guilt at being alive at all.'
Now to after the war and the Falkland Islanders themselves. Their
whole lives were disrupted but today many of their livelihoods
revolve solely around the presence of the armed forces. Many are
no better off than before the war, regardless of the fact that the
financial costs so far have resulted in about £2 million per Falkland
Islander being spent.

And finally to the future. With Britain's arms trade benefiting
substantially from the war, one can only assume that the suffering
from the war will extend for decades.

Dr G.A. Makin: I wanted to explain that the return of the
Argentine dead is a very sensitive subject in Argentina. However
President Alfonsin has given Mr Gimenez, chair of the Education
Committee every assurance that it is not government policy to
prevent interment of the bodies, this was stated several times by
the Prime Minister. In fact there is no way legally in which these
people can be prevented from either travelling to the Islands or
returning, and this is the crucial word, returning bodies to a point
closer to the address of their parents. And there is a substantial
indication that that is not Argentine policy, President Alfonsin
signed executive orders whereby Malvinas Argentinas, the official
airline, did not charge Mr Gimenez for his trip to Europe.

Joan Hymans: The first question relates to the Merchant Seamen
who were on the supply ships. In my recollection they had to stay
there a great deal longer than their contracts were for and this was
costing their families a very considerable sum. I remember that
there were tremendous protests against their not being even
allowed onto the Island, they had to stay in the ships, and I wonder
whether the cost which has been reckoned includes any
compensation. Whether they were paid any compensation?

And the second question is, it struck me as the time of the Victory
Parade that it had been deliberately arranged for the time when
the Queen was at the Commonwealth Games out of the country
and this must have been known years in advance. Has Mrs
Thatcher ever been asked why that was the fact and I understand
that even the Palace was not invited to send anybody else?

Wade Tidbury: Now on the point that you made about the
Merchant Seamen I'd suggest that after the war for many months
very few civilians from outside the Falklands were actually allowed
onto the Falkland Islands themselves. This was for several good
reasons, one is that there were many mines which had been laid
during the war and many unexploded bombs lying around and
people once they got onto the Falklands were looking for

souvenirs. This did cause some injuries to people. This did cause
a few problems because people were getting hands and legs blown
off after the war and it was causing a lot of embarrassment for the
authorities. That could be the explanation as to why they weren't
allowed onto the Island. As to the costs to the wives back home,
I couldn't comment because I don't really know anything about
that other than what you've just said.

But with reference to the Victory Parade I doubt if they'd have
known years in advance but perhaps a few months in advance
about the date of the Parade. The date of the Parade I think was
geared to be a couple of weeks after the return of the Invincible
although I am perhaps wrong there. But they wanted to include
some men from each of the contingents that went down there.

Joan Hymans: The Queen was there when her son came back.
Then why didn't they have the Victory Parade at that time?

Wade Tidbury: I'm not sure, but we can all but guess can't we?

Ian MacPhail: It's my recollection that, I think it was through
the E.E.C. action, that President Mitterand or somebody in
France as important, was persuaded not to complete the delivery
of Exocets to the Argentines. If that is correct I'd like Dr Rogers
just to speculate on what might have happened if that hadn't
happened bearing in mind that the Argentine pilots were very
skilled pilots.

Paul Rogers: As far as is known at the start of the conflict
Argentina had only about five Exocet missiles available for arming
the Super Etendard plane. They were in the process of equipping
a full squadron with these planes and with missiles to go with them.
They had undergone a lot of training in France, the pilots
themselves, and they were at the point where they could certainly
use the missiles that they had available. If more had been made
available, and they went to very considerable efforts to try and
get Exocets from part of the International arms market, then
obviously they would have been able to conduct far more sorties
against Task Force ships and the consequences could have been
extremely serious. It's worth bearing in mind that although we
commonly describe the Exocet as a French missile it is actually
Franco-British. The Royal Navy is very widely equipped with the
Exocet and parts of the components are in fact made in Britain.
Incidentally the refitting of the Argentine navy and the re-
equipment with new ships in fact since the war has involved
considerable British equipment. The Type 3/400 Destroyer is
actually powered by Rolls Royce engines, the gear boxes are
David Brown and the control systems are Hawker Sidley, and
some of the contracts have actually been completed since the war
was ended.

Wade Tidbury: If I could just comment on that, I've got a very ironic position that I could convey to you. A girl friend who was writing to me while I was in the Falklands works for Plessey Connectors of Northampton. They have a contract with the company which makes Exocet missiles. In one of her letters she mentioned the massive amount of overtime she was suddenly being asked to do and 'We're doing the fleet proud,' she said. The orders were being sent out to France. If the Argentines only had five Exocet missiles I want to know why we in the fleet saw at least 10 on our radar screens? Just having the idea that someone who I knew was making something which was being exported and used against me to kill me, just shows up the horrors of the arms trade.

Paul Rogers: I should make the point that the figure of five is the figure officially given. There have been a number of unofficial reports that Argentina had more and in fact may have acquired some during the war.

Bill Hawthorne: Paul Rogers has described the creation of Fortress Falklands and quantified some of the money involved. I wonder whether much is known about lucrative defence contracts awarded to people in the U.K. and do you feel that there is an industrial lobby which has a vested interest in postponing a peaceful settlement of the Falklands issue?

Paul Rogers: Well broadly speaking obviously there is a very powerful industrial lobby in Britain. They interlink, say the nuclear and the non-nuclear lobby, and there are many obviously major defence firms who are keen on the development of new contracts. And I wouldn't say that there is one particular lobby which is just concerned with Fortress Falklands but obviously the Falklands policy with particular certain sorts of equipment, surface and air-search radar for example, the arms lobby would find the expenditure on Fortress Falklands a useful part of the whole process. I'm not aware of any specific lobby in that sense but I think it forms part of a wider situation.

Wade Tidbury: Can I again come in. It would perhaps be worth looking at, and I have done on a number of occasions, the names of the companies which contribute to certain political parties leading up to election times and the names of the companies which appear on the Falkland Islands contract. I'd also suggest that they're very similar to the names of the companies which appear on the contracts for building such areas as Greenham Common and Molesworth and so on.

Bill Hetherington: First actually I would like just to make one correction to Wade's very moving contribution but since it is important to establish facts I think it ought to be put into the record that the first deaths arising from the war did not actually occur as a result of the raiding on Port Stanley and Goose Green. They actually occurred on South Georgia, it was a loss of Argentinians. It occurred I think actually during the Argentinian invasion of South Georgia and there may also have been further loss of life on the re-invasion of Georgia by the British Forces. But certainly it was in South Georgia the first loss of life occurred not actually on the Falkland Islands proper, so I think that ought to be written into the record.

But my main question was for Diana. It was obviously appropriate to recall the number of deaths not only on the British but also on the Argentinian side during the war itself. But I am raising what to me are the most poignant deaths of all throughout the war, the deaths of three Islanders killed by the Royal Navy, have not been mentioned at all. And I ask Diana why in fact that very serious ommission has been made, both in the Handbook when the figures are set down and also in her contribution, because I think that is fundamental when looking at the war. That the war was supposed to save 1800 Islanders and three of them were actually killed by the forces. They were killed by shelling on the shore. I can't remember exactly where, I think it was somewhere in the neighbourhood of Port Stanley but I can't remember exactly but they were definately killed by the Royal Navy. The matter was published at the time by the British press but I gather from the audience here a number of people are entirely unaware that Islanders were actually killed by the Royal Navy.

Diana Gould: Well I think somewhere I did say the dead of both sides including civilians. But it is perfectly true what you say that they were killed during the final stages of the war with the shelling of Port Stanley. And according to, I think it's the Sunday Times Insight Team, their book on the Falkland Islands, Wade may know a bit more about this, but the captain of whichever ship it was that did it, came to see the people because he was horrified because he'd been told that there were no people in a certain section. They had no idea that there where still people in that area of Stanley. I believe you'll find that in the Falklands book by the Sunday Times Insight Team. But it is fact that the only Islanders that did die were killed by us, that is certainly a fact.

I don't know if anybody has felt that I attacked the Islanders. All I'm trying to say to them is do they realise the responsibility put upon them? But I would like just to add a little here. There is a book which is supposed to be one of the definitive studies of the Falkland Islands, I'm not talking about the war now, I'm talking about the Falkland Islands, and it is written by an Islander who lived through the whole of the Falklands incident. I don't know who he is and I honestly cannot tell you, perhaps someone might enlighten me here, what he does on the Islands. His name is Ian J Strange and he wrote this book called 'The Falkland Islands' in the 1970s. It covers every aspect you can possibly think about from the history through to the ecology, the geology, anything, you'll find it in that book. He revised it in early 1982, because it was revised before the war, and the third edition, which is the one that I got hold of, was revised by him in 1983 to include a section on the war and of course it is written from the viewpoint of an Islander. I would like to read one bit of his conclusion at the end of his book, page 310; this is the conclusion of an Islander, a man who's lived there all his life and as I say a man who is obviously an authority on the whole thing, and he says this:

'There has to be a peaceful and definitive solution to the present situation which geographical fact dictates must have some connection with Argentina in the future. It is difficult in the long term to visualise a situation which does not involve the United Nations, perhaps in some form of trusteeship in the larger framework of a multinational treaty.'

And that is an Islander who obviously thinks a great deal but it is very interesting to see that he says there must be some connection with Argentina in any final solution that's going to occur.

Eric Ogden: There are two recent books written by the Islanders about the Islands. Ian Strange is the artist or ecologist, naturalist, philatelist who wrote the addition to his book on the Falkland Islands after the war. The second book that has been written by an Islander, a diary of the war, is by John Smith, formerly of the British Atlantic Survey, an artist, a cartographer and an enthusiast, and that book is called '74 Days'. It's a diary of the Islanders' experience in Stanley during the war.

If I can ask a question of Diana Gould first. Would she please direct her efforts to help get Argentine families to visit the graves at Goose Green and Darwin through the International Red Cross, not the Argentine Red Cross. Unfortunately, during the occupation, representatives of the Argentine Red Cross visited the Islands to supposedly see what the conditions were like for the Islanders under the occupation. One Islander told me he felt rather like an inhabitant of Auchwitz being visited by the S.S. So they are not regarded by the Islanders as neutral. I hope perhaps the churches would help in this regard but if the efforts are made only through the Argentine Red Cross you will have great difficulty. The churches are probably the best ones to do this.

May I try to respond to the question Diana Gould made. She said 'Do the Islanders know the cost of war?' They do. As a gentleman at the front said, three Islanders were also killed. I spoke in the debate in the House of Commons, the very short question and answer debate immediately when that announcement was made. Those three Islanders I was proud to call my friends. No one in the Islands blamed the British forces. The Islanders are aware of the cost of the war but the question is like saying to a victim of robbery or rape, 'Are you aware of the cost of the Police Force?' If the platform had been in Stanley Cathedral on the anniversairy celebrations they would have heard the final words of the Rector of Stanley about the invasion. If I remember them rightly, 'To these fair Islands our fathers came to raise their children and their sheep in a peaceful country. We bear for ever in our minds the memory of those our brothers from afar who came to us in that darkest hour.' So the Falkland Islanders know the price that was paid. In the last war as in the first they have made their contribution and their sacrifices for us.

Helen Trask: Tam Dalyell says that the Falklands have no strategic importance. I have been told that they do because of the importance of the Antarctic. I would just like to know if Dr Rogers thinks that there was any strategic importance which would define part of the motive for keeping the Falkland Islands?

Paul Rogers: I think that the strategic importance of the Falklands is pretty mimimal. The Cape Horn sea route is a relatively minor, in fact a very minor sea route. The South African Cape route is an extremely important route but the Falkland Islands are about 4,000 miles away in the wrong place. They're in the South West Atlantic whereas the Cape of Good Hope route is in the South East Atlantic and you have a huge stretch of water in between. If you could tow the Falkland Islands to the north east then they would become strategically important in that context. There is very little importance strategically in terms of world East-West relations as to where the Falkland Islands are now. They're so close to the Latin American mainland.

If indeed you could consider any strategic importance in an East-West context, then what would be crucial would be to get a peaceful settlement with Argentina. Because if you are saying that they are strategically important then what you don't want is to be in conflict with your immediate neighbour.

As far as Antarctica is concerned one could certainly say that the Falklands are important as a kind of jumping-off area for the Antarctic. But I think the really crucial thing about the Antarctic is that it is that rarity on the globe, a non-militarised zone, and long may it remain so. HMS Endurance, if it goes on ice patrol below a certain latitude, actually shrouds its guns because it is entering a non-military area. And there has been a remarkable level of cooperation among many countries in terms of the exploration of Antarctica. There are conflicts as well over the territories but those have not in any way yet resorted to military conflict. I think what is important is to avoid the military conflict which we've had in the South Atlantic spilling over into Antarctica. In my view that makes it even more important to get some sort of agreed settlement.

Wade Tidbury: I think Helen was right when she suggested the Falklands do have a strategic importance. Given the way countries disregard treaties when their own financial gains come in to importance, I would suggest that upon the discovery of mineral wealth and oil in the Antarctic regions there will be an all-out bonanza, there will be oil fields and there will be exploitation on a scale I don't think we've see before. So the Falkland Islands will then become, as Paul suggested, a jumping-off point for the Antarctic regions and I think that's something we have to consider for the future.

Helen Trask: May I ask one more point on that? Is it a fact that the United States already has some men, some force or other, on the airfield which has been built there? I heard that just recently in connection with their attitude to the South American States. The suggestion was that they might feel that would be a good base for them because they have no other base as far south as that?

Paul Rogers: The United States certainly has, and has had for a long time, close links with Chile. There have been Signals Intelligence Stations up in Chile. Before the Falklands war there was certainly a signalling facility on the Falklands which linked in with wireless facilities. I don't think there was direct U.S. personnel involved. I'm not aware that there are U.S. personnel involved now, but I could be mistaken on that. But certainly the Falklands was a link, one very small part of a global network.

Helen Trask: But it's now got this enormous airfield.

Paul Rogers: The Signals Intelligence Facilities may well have been built up. I'm not aware of any direct U.S. personnel stationed there but I could be wrong.

Duncan Smith: Could I ask Paul Rogers whether anything specific is known about the possible oil resources of the area?

Paul Rogers: Not really, it is one of the lesser sedimentary deposits, the area between the Islands and the mainland. There is belief that there could be quite reasonable oil reserves which might be exploitable, if not with present technology, maybe with future technology. The problem here and you see it a little bit in the dispute over the fisheries is that the continuing quite grievous dispute between Britain and Argentina actually makes the safe exploitation of the resources much more difficult. You have had something of a free-for-all on the fishery side and you're unlikely to get investment in development of oil reserves as long as the present conflict continues. The major companies are unlikely to invest in offshore exploration and development while we have this conflict continuing. So once again you have the paradox in that the exploitation of the reserves of the Southwest Atlantic are to a large extent conditional on getting a settlement to the present dispute.

Denis Ridgeway: When it was said earlier about the wounded not being visible during the Victory Parade, I would like in fact to make a very brief statement that certainly there are other aspects of this as well. My sister who lives in Canada came over to meet with us shortly after the Falklands war and said, 'What did you think about the pictures on television of the wounded arriving back in the U.K. from the Falklands?' which they had seen pictures of in Canada. Now I was watching the broadcasts very conscientiously during this period and I don't remember seeing pictures here and I have a very strong feeling that this was intentional and it is in keeping with the same spirit that was present when the wounded were not made visible and they didn't wish them to be visible. I would like to make one further point: this session is called 'Cost of the War' and bearing in mind that large numbers of servicemen from this country were killed and wounded, the losses in terms of life were rather disproportionate in relation to the losses that were suffered by the Falklanders. And the phrase that the wishes of the Islanders should be paramount, I sometimes wonder whether this view should be maintained bearing in mind there must be other wishes that the Islanders have.

Malcolm Dando: I've been surprised that we've spent so little time talking about the Haig mission. We've referred to it in passing but we haven't looked at it in any great detail. And I just wonder if Paul could say a little bit more about the U.S. connection in terms of cost, particularly because of that Economist article, a very detailed Economist article which suggested that there was a great deal of material coming from the U.S.A. to Britain before the United States officially tilted towards us. If this was as big an input into our victory as was suggested in the Economist article are there any possible consequences of that?

Paul Rogers: I think one of the things one has to recognise is the nature of internal U.S. politics in April and May 1982. The Secretary of State at the time, General Haig, was extremely pro-British. There were other elements of the Reagan administration who were far less so — Jean Kirkpatrick in particular, the U.S. representative at the United Nations. There was obviously quite a considerable conflict which developed within the administration as to the extent of the support for the United

Kingdom. I've talked at length to a current state department man, quite a senior man who was on Kirkpatrick's staff during the war and it certainly is clear that this conflict continued. What I think is very important is that Haig carried more weight than Kirkpatrick and much more important still were the huge number of connections between the British armed forces and the American armed forces.

It's certainly true that a wide variety of material was made available. The United Stated did not quibble at the use of the Wide Awake facility on Ascension Island which became briefly the world's busiest airport during the course of the Falklands war, whereas previously it might have one plane every fortnight. And in certain areas the U.S. support was absolutely crucial. Probably the most important single area — again it's almost an abstruse technical issue — is that the anti-aircraft missiles with which the British carriers and Sea Harriers were equipped were the so-called 'Side-winder' missiles and the maker of this missile in the United States, a very widely used missile, had come up with a very much improved version which was incredibly sensitive in terms of it's heat-seeking ability. Britain had some supplies of this at the start of the war. It was realised they would very quickly be exhausted. And the United States provided large numbers of the 'Side-winder' Mark-L which were used throughout the war and contributed hugely to the success of the Harriers in maintaining some degree of air superiority over the Islands. Now that was evidently occurring before as well as after the Belgrano incident and really privately there was a huge flow of equipment and material across the Atlantic throughout the war. There were very close links but it's worth pointing out there were differences of opinion with the Reagan administration. The military links in fact prevailed.

Duncan Smith: I should like to follow up Denis Ridgeway's point and ask Paul Rogers whether his school has made any study of the treatment of the Falklands situation by the media, particularly the television, and whether it is still continuing to do so? Because in respect of this enquiry we had expressions of great interest by senior people from Channel 4 but when it came to the point no action has been taken to give any coverage whatever. Norman Tebbit has obviously scared the BBC rigid and we therefore didn't expect any coverage from them. Is there any particular study being made on this rather important point?

Paul Rogers: Not by our department. We don't actually specialise to any great extent in media studies. We're more likely to be looking at the conflicts themselves, how they arise and how they might be resolved. Quite a major book on the coverage of the

Falklands war was written by the Glasgow Media Group, 'War and Peace News' which was published about a year ago. We had one of our students, a German student, who did a piece of work in the final year of her degree on the treatment of the war by the West German media, which in fact is an intriguing study. Basically it showed a sequence: for the first month of the war the West German media regarded the conflict as almost something of a joke. It seemed extraordinary that countries could come to blows over this particular issue. After the sinking of the Belgrano they took it very much more seriously and regarded it as quite an extraordinary episode in terms of the resources which Britain was putting into the war. They seemed to regard it as though the country had taken leave of its senses in terms of getting everything absolutely out of proportion. The interesting thing is that that was broadly across the political spectrum in West Germany, from Right through to Left in terms of the media.

It's true to say that our own experience in doing analyses of the war and its aftermath have tended to get much more coverage overseas than in Britain. And I'm talking about Canada, the United States, Belgium, Sweden, Holland and such countries. The media interest in Britain is rather low except when you get some sort of major controversy as happened with the arrest of Clive Ponting.

Intervention from the floor: I would just like to say that I was in Germany at the time of the Falklands war and actually the German public were just angry about the whole thing. It wasn't just a question of laughing at it, they were angry and bitter that England was still trying to assert its need for a colonial past. And they were angry because they didn't think Britain had that right, the right to invade the Falklands and to make it a major conflict. The media at the time were very clear to reflect that and they made a major documentary at the time because they were just angry and bitter really....

Jean Woolf: Could I just say something which involves Diana, which is that when Diana was interviewed by somebody at the Times, unfortunately I've forgotten his name, he came to us and he said 'I really want to interview Diana, this remarkable lady.' And we said, 'Fine,' and we gave him her address and he went down and interviewed her. He came back to us very apologetically because she'd given him a very good lunch and we thought it marvellous, you know, Diana's book will actually be known to the public, and he said, 'I can't get it in'. They say, "The Belgrano! We can't do anything on the Belgrano."' I thought that was very interesting at the time and very significant. I mean given that it was the Times we can obviously understand why, but even the

Guardian talked about Tam's Belgrano War and folk getting bored. I think the media's reacted very strongly to the whole incident of the Belgrano.

Dr Makin: I would just like to refer everybody to the official study that was in fact commissioned by the M.O.D. on the media. It reflects surprising opinions for an officially commissioned study in terms of mismanagement and censorship. Even after I read an M.O.D. censored version the admission that censorship had been used on several paragraphs by British official apparatus is quite astounding.

Wade Tidbury: Two of the correspondents working for, I believe it's the B.B.C., in the Falklands, Brian Hanrahan and Robert Fox, both expressed their own professional frustrations about the restrictions that the Ministry of Defence placed upon them on reporting certain issues. In their own words they were in conflict with the Ministry of Defence about restrictions on the way that news was reported. I could refer to the situation after the Alacrity had sunk an Argentinian ship in the Falkland Sound, it was an advantage for the Ministry of Defence to actually name our ship as the ship which sunk the Argentinian ship, which was against all policy. It was a very dangerous thing to do and I can remember our captain being visibly angry that the Ministry of Defence should do this, whilst being incapable of reporting other aspects of the conflict. So it was the Ministry of Defence who were manipulating the media and are still doing now.

Richard Baker: This is an episode which a lot of people might find embarassing and just don't want to know and want to forget about it. Is that carelessness or has anybody studied, as far as you can study, whether public opinion has..

Paul Rogers: I'm not aware of any major studies done since the war. Obviously a lot of studies on how opinion developed during the war, the way in which public opinion moved increasingly behind the Government in the later stages of the war, but was not at the start of the war. That shows clearly if you look at the sequence of the polls conducted during the war. For example one major poll conducted for the Sunday Times, conducted I think on April 30th, published paradoxically on the day that the Belgrano was to be sunk, that actually showed that only one in seven of those polled in Britain thought that the Falklands conflict was sufficiently serious to warrant the risking of 100 or more lives. So the overwhelming proportion of people did not think that it was sufficiently serious to risk many lives.

Taggart Deike: I'm Taggart Deike, member of Equity for Nuclear Disarmament. I wrote a play about the Falklands war soon after the Falklands war, sort of a review piece which we performed here in Hampstead. But the thing is that we looked very carefully at that time for material for our review, right? We weren't getting it, it was exceedingly difficult to get it and in fact the interesting thing was when we talked to people, that after years and years of live footage from all over the world about the Vietnam war, here we were watching television night and day and all we were getting were mockups from the studio. The whole thing was controlled, absolutely controlled. The information came out of all our interviews with Denis Healey and David Owen and so on. Now you mention Brian Hanrahan, Brian Hanrahan was allowed some time after the war to do his story about his scoop. He had a scoop about the last battle of the war and he then told in this particular story, post Falklands story, of the problems that they had generally in getting those stories through. They had to go to a special ship and there, an officer on board that ship would have to approve everything. In this particular incident Brian Hanrahan had the scoop of the war, the war was over, and all he wanted to do was get back to his editor. A., he had a hell of a time getting there because we were actually blocking him from getting there, and B., when he actually got there the officer said, 'I'm not letting it through.' And Hanrahan was livid, he said 'Why? There's nothing to do with security here.' He said 'Well no, absolutely not.' So even when they had the story, even when it was a scoop, they weren't allowed to print it through the press. This is vital and important censorship.

Wade Tidbury: If I may quote from a section in Brian Hanrahan's book, about being a war correspondent,

'But apart from the delayed copy and the cut out of words, there were deeper problems reflecting the role of the free press. Bad news was instinctively delayed, when HMS Sheffield was lost the news was banned and only later released in London under intense pressure. None of us wanted to tell the dreadful story but it was important that it should come from the British side first. If Argentina had announced it first only to have it confirmed by the British later, then every future Argentine claim would cause untold anguish at home. It's a principle that journalists hold to, that accurate news should be released unimpeded, it strengthens the credibility of both correspondent and the organisation he's reporting on. It's the ability to tell the truth even when it hurts and we think it sets democracies apart. Instead we were faced with constant restraints and restrictions which slowed and diminished our reporting. It seemed to have more to do with bureaucratic infighting in the Ministry of Defence than security.

The fact that Vulcans had bombed Port Stanley was supposed to be a state secret on one ship. On mine I was told it was an R.A.F. matter and shouldn't be released through naval channels. I don't think anyone objected to the censoring of our military material, detail which might help the enemy, after all our lives were at risk as much as anybody elses. And with the local military command there would be difficulties. We did not report what they asked us not to. But the detailed censoring was left to civilian public relations men whose instructions came from London and often seemed at odds with the local command. Sometimes the policy dictated from London seemed two-faced. While we withheld details of unexploded bombs for very good reasons, that the Argentines might re-examine the fuses, highly accurate accounts were appearing in the newspapers, accounts which could only have come from within the Ministry of Defence. While we were only reporting past events, the attacks on Darwin and the surrender of Goose Green were leaked before they happened. While we stayed silent about unopposed military advances, somebody announced in London that we were moving along the North Coast long before there was evidence that the Argentines had even detected it.

So far I've been talking in general terms about all journalism. But my particular job was reporting television, and in television terms this was the unreported war. There is no doubt that the military satellite system can carry television pictures, but no pictures have been sent back. Not even a test transmission has been authorised. It's hard to believe that in no time during the 10 weeks could we find time to show a little of what was happening, especially when world opinion was so important to Britain.'

VII

Lessons of the War for the Future

Ian Mikardo, John Madeley, Malcolm Harper, Michael
Harbottle, Eric Ogden

Ian Mikardo

I base what I have to say on the Minority Report presented by the
four Labour members of the Select Committee of Foreign Affairs
on the Committee's study of events surrounding the weekend of
1st/2nd May 1982. The weekend in which the Peruvian peace
proposals were canvassed; the weekend in which our Foreign
Secretary was in the United States engaged in talks about a
diplomatic solution of the conflict between Great Britain and the
Argentine; and the weekend in which the cruiser Belgrano was
sunk with such very heavy loss of life. That Minority Report
contains a great deal of material and in the time that is available
to me I will have to be strictly selective and concentrate on only
one or two of the points we brought up. We were so conscious of
the limitations placed upon the results we could get that the main
conclusion of our Minority Report was that we called for another
inquiry, for a high level inquiry perhaps on Privy Council terms,
to discover what we had been unable to uncover. And we'd been
unable to uncover many things, in some cases because the majority
of the Select Committee refused to ask some questions that ought
to have been asked and in other cases, either because the
Government refused to answer some of the questions they were
asked or because they answered those questions at best
misleadingly and at worse untruthfully. In Section 9 of the
Minority Report we listed 30 such questions. Until those questions
are answered, and one day they will be, the full truth about the
Falklands war will be hidden from the people of Britain and from
the world.

Section 7 of our report set out the seven later lies which the
Government told the House of Commons and the nation. I quote
shortly four passages to indicate the width and depth of the
deception. Paragraph 7.16 of our Minority Report:

'Although it may have been considered necessary during the
conflict for certain facts not to be revealed on genuine
grounds of national security, this is no excuse for a minister

knowingly to make a false statement to Parliament. Nor
does it explain the perpetuation of the substance of John
Nott's misstatements for so long after the event. We deplore
the deception of Parliament, the failure of Her Majesty's
Government to correct false statements at the earliest
opportunity and the subsequent reiteration of untrue or
misleading statements by Government ministers. If ministers
are allowed to treat Parliament in such a manner then it
seriously undermines the accountability of the executive to
the House of Commons which is one of the essentials of our
Parliamentary democracy.'

And then a couple of paragraphs later,

'It is clear from the Secretary of State's evidence that in late
March and early April 1984 he made a conscious decision to
withold certain information from Members, not because its
release would itself be detrimental to national interest but
because it could supposedly lead to further requests for
information.'

They didn't answer questions for fear that we might ask some more.
And then we go on later.

'We are satisfied that the main reason for Her Majesty's
Government's reluctance to give the Committee information
was not on grounds of national security. It had more to do
with the Government's desire not to release the full and true
information which would be inconsistent with previous
ministerial statements and would therefore embarrass the
Government.'

And then we conclude,

'We are of the opinion that national security was used as a
convenient smokescreen to protect the credibility of the
Government. We therefore absolutely condemn the
Goverment's deliberate attempt to obstruct a legitimate
enquiry by a Parliamentary Select Committee which had the
right to enquire and get truthful answers. It was clearly the
intention of ministers to provide the Committee with a
memorandum which would be not only misleading but which
was intended to block any further enquiries.'

But the basic deception, the basic deception from which all the
rest flows, the basic deception which we did manage to uncover
in spite of deliberate ministerial obstruction, was that a week
before the critical Belgrano weekend, the Government decided
to make a radical change in their announced Falklands policy.
They decided at the same time to deceive the House and the
country by not announcing the change and by pretending that they
were continuing the original stated policy. That original stated

policy was to use the minimum force necessary to secure a diplomatic solution to the conflict. During the weekend of 23rd/24th April the War Cabinet decided to abandon that policy and they decided instead to carry out an act of aggression sufficiently large and dramatic to precipitate and to escalate military action to the level that they could impose a solution by force. The large and dramatic act which they chose was to sink the aircraft carrier Veinticinco de Mayo which they could reasonably claim was a potential source of danger to our forces. So they searched the seas for the aircraft carrier but even with all the American satellites and G.C.H.Q. and all the rest of it, they failed to find the aircraft carrier. But they had to have some target, so instead they sank the Belgrano which they knew perfectly well was not a potential source of danger to our forces. The question, "Why did we sink the Belgrano?" has been asked many times and has had many different answers. But it is clear from our researches that the sure and absolute factual answer to the question, "Why did we sink the Belgrano?" is, we sank the Belgrano because we couldn't find the Veinticinco de Mayo.

The visit of Francis Pym to Washington and New York over the weekend of the 1st and 2nd May was part of the pretence that the Government was still seeking a diplomatic solution. Mind you, he himself, Francis himself was not a party to the deception, indeed he was one of the victims of it. He was sent off, an innocent abroad, to talk peace with Al Haig and Perez de Cuellar without being told that any such talk would be scuppered while he was engaged in it, by the decision to sink one of the Argentine capital ships. We got to know about this because, in the last meeting with the United States Secretary of State, he sounded out what would be Her Majesty's Government's reaction to a proposal for a further cease-fire of a few days in order to seek further negotiations and a solution by diplomatic means. The answer he got was that the Government would not do anything that limited its military options. That is a clear indication that they were no longer, as they pretended they were, seeking a diplomatic solution.

How do we know about this? After that last interview the then British Ambassador reported that interview by Telex to the Foreign and Commonwealth Office. We were only able to see that Telex because we succeeded, after much pressure and in spite of much resistance to get a look at what was called The Crown Jewels, the document which Clive Ponting prepared at Michael Heseltine's request to inform Heseltine of what had happened. The Crown Jewels contained a lot of information which it was quite proper to keep confidential, there was a lot of stuff in it about Rules of Engagement and signals, and it was fair enough on security grounds to keep that confidential. And therefore we weren't allowed to have that document. What we were allowed to do was to go along to the Ministry of Defence and sit down and read it. We were forbidden even to make notes in order to be able to use anything. We had to reply entirely on our memory for anything that we wanted to use. They bound into that document the Ambassador's Telex. It had nothing to do with that document, it had nothing to do with Rules of Engagement or signals, and we were then told that that Telex was confidential, not on security grounds because there was nothing in it about security, but because it had been bound in the same file as documents which were confidential on security grounds. Nevertheless we now know what is in it and we can make use of what is in it, and what is in it is the statement that Her Majesty's Government's reaction to the suggestion of another short period of a few days of cease-fire to try and reach a negotiated solution was that they wouldn't accept anything that limited their military options.

Finally I'd like to say a word on the question whether the Government knew of the Peruvian Peace Plan before the Belgrano was sunk. We delved a lot into this and we deliberated a lot about it and the conclusion, or perhaps I could say non-conclusion, to which we came, is set out in paragraph 5.16 of the Minority Report, in which we say this:

'The possibility of a link between the Peruvian Peace Initiative and the sinking of the Belgrano is still an open question. The Goverment's suppression of evidence and giving of false evidence throughout the whole of this affair make it risky to base a firm conclusion on what they have said and that is one reason why we would recommend a further inquiry.'

In support of their case the Government rests solely on detente between the then British Ambassador in Lima and the Peruvian Foreign Minister and they have asserted that that was the only *official* contact between the two goverments over that period. But the purport of the word official, the only official contact, the purport of the word official in that context is to suggest that there was also some unofficial contact. What was it? That's a question which must be asked. What was it? Did it involved Lord Thomas? During the debate in the House of Lords. Lord Hatch asked that very question, was Lord Thomas involved in unofficial contacts prior to and during that weekend? Lord Hatch asked that question and notified Lord Thomas in advance that he was going to ask it. After that prior notification Lord Thomas significantly and studiously absented himself from that debate. It must surely be a prima facie assumption that if he were not involved in any way he would have gone along to the House to say so. That's why Number 9 of the 30 questions we want a further inquiry to answer is this:

'In addition to official communications, what information if any about the Peruvian Peace Initiative did the Prime Minister or other ministers receive from other sources, including the United States Embassy in Lima or sources in Britain or elsewhere?'

One day, as I've said, we'll get all those questions answered. I hope I shall still be around.

John Madeley

The name Diego Garcia may not convey a great deal to many people. Until a few years ago many were uncertain whether it was a person or a place, but it is in fact an island in the Indian Ocean, one of a group of Islands which make up the Chagos Islands. It's about 2,000 miles from Mauritius and just over 1,000 miles from India, it's right in the heart of the Indian Ocean. And there is a very definite link between the way the people of Diego Garcia were treated and the way the Falkland Islanders were treated. And indeed more than that, a link in the chain of events that one can see from March 1982. Before I mention that, I'd just like to explain very briefly one or two common characteristics that the two groups of islands have, the Falklands and the Chagos Islands. Both were colonised by Britain in the early years of the 1900s at about the same time, and 20 years ago both had a similar population of about 1800 people. The contrast in one sense ends there. The Falkland Islanders were white, the people of the Chagos Islands were the descendents of African slaves, leprosy settlers, a very mixed race. They go under the name of the Ilois and I will refer to them, as this is the French name for Islanders, I will refer to them like that.

In the 1950s the colonial office made a film about them which said what a glorious life they led and referred to them being born and bred on the islands. That turned out to be very important in the light of subsequent events. In 1965 the British Government, the then Labour Government, had talks with the American Government about the possibility of leasing Diego Garcia to the United States first of all as a so-called 'communications facility'. It was intended to monitor the activities of the Soviet Navy. The talks moved to a successful completion and Britain agreed that the island of Diego Garcia, an island in the Chagos Islands should be leased to the American Government for a period of 50 years. But there was a snag. America made it quite clear that it did not want any natives on that island and the natives had to go. About this time Britain was also engaged in giving Mauritius independence and the Chagos Islands were historically part of Mauritius. And we agreed to give Mauritius independence on condition that we kept sovereignty over the Chagos Islands. There was quite a hotly disputed debate in Mauritius about this but finally that was agreed to and Mauritius was given independence in 1968. And an agreement was signed in 1966, signed for Britain by George Brown, to lease the islands to America for 50 years, purely as a support facility, not a base as it has now turned out to be.

However, Britain had the job of getting rid of these people that America didn't want and between 1965 and 1973 it systematically drained the islands of the Ilois people. It did this by what I think can only be regarded as a most inhuman way. People had often gone to Mauritius, they did have close family links with Mauritius, they'd often gone there to see family and friends. And what happened, and nobody knew about this until some years after, is that when people, when the Ilois wanted to return home to Diego Garcia and the other islands, they were told there were no boats available to take them home. No return boats were allowed to leave and the people were left to fend as best they could in Mauritius with their family and friends. And that went on until 1973. In fact there was quite a large evacuation in 1971 just as the Americans were coming in.

Now no one knew anything about this. These people were the living victims of our secretive system of government. The first time that the crime really became known was when an American journalist exposed it in September 1975 for the Washington Post. The Sunday Times followed it up with an excellent exposé on the 21st September 1975, 'The Islanders that Britain Sold'. What lay behind the title is that in fact we obtained a small discount on Polaris submarines from the United States for selling the islanders, selling them out.

No compensation whatsoever had been paid to them at this stage. They hadn't had a penny. They were promised jobs apparently on Mauritius, but Mauritius is an island with poverty and unemployment of its own and most of them simply didn't get jobs. They were living in very harrowing circumstances. They appealed for compensation, Britain said it would give three quarters of a million pounds. It was totally inadequate and throughout the late 1970s the plight of these people went on and Britain refused to give compensation of any significant amount.

All this changed quite dramatically in 1982. Having done nothing about compensation for 17 years, nothing very significant — I think by that time they had increased their offer to an amount totalling about one and a half million pounds — the British

Government suddenly at the end of March increased its offer. The reason for that, in my opinion and this is only my opinion and no one will ever know until the full facts become known, lies in the emerging Falklands conflict. On March 5th the Prime Minister made some preliminary plans for attacking the Falklands, or for regaining the Falklands as you have said. That was on March 5th. On March 20th a British team of officials flew to Mauritius with a vastly increased offer of compensation. They doubled the previous offer which was about one and a half million pounds to three million pounds. It was an action totally unprecedented and could not be forseen in any way, based on the way they'd treated these people in the past 17 years. The Ilois people said, 'No it is not enough'. The British Government immediately raised its offer to four million pounds and that was accepted. On March 27th the deal was signed. Five days later Argentina invaded the Falklands and the rest you know.

Why I suggest there's a link is simply this. These people were British subjects: they were living in a British colony the way the people of the Falkland Islands were, they were treated so very differently and so disgracefully from the Falkland Islanders. How could Britain possibly have taken action as it did on the Falklands, if it had the people of Diego Garcia hanging around its neck still treating them so badly? It had in my view to make some kind of accommodation. It had to meet some of their claims. They were asking for eight million pounds, they settled for four million pounds. They had to make what appeared to be a reasonable contract otherwise the double standard between the way the Ilois people and the Falkland Islanders were being treated, the double standard would have been so stark, that I don't think Britain'a position on the Falklands would have been credible. I think there would have been far more questions and therefore they had to make this deal with the Ilois people. And that money was eventually given and the position of the islanders has since improved a little. But what they went through in those years has I think left so deep a scar, that no amount of money will really heal what they've suffered. And I am afraid that they have suffered at the hands of the British Government. Now Britain was very keen when we took the Falklands action to point out that the instigators of aggression could not be allowed to get away with it. Fine. That should apply elsewhere and the British Government has practised aggression, I'm sorry to say, against the Ilois for many years.

Macolm Harper
Yesterday morning we spoke particularly about whether or not the

United Kingdom in the wake of Resolution 502 made adequate use of the United Nations as the machine through which to try to find a diplomatic solution to the conflict. I'd like if I may in summarising British policy towards the United Nations to read briefly just one short paragraph from the Sunday Times Insight Team book on the Falklands war, and this is what they say, written about events in the United Nations over the weekend of the 1st/2nd May 1982:

> 'Meanwhile events had moved to the United Nations where Britain's diplomatic efforts had been bent with great single-mindedness towards one simple aim, keeping the Falklands issue out of the Security Council. Having won Resolution 502 the British knew that if they ever went back to the Security Council they would almost certainly be presented with something far less effective. "There was nothing more we could get from the Council", said one British official. "Our job was to keep them at bay. There were a few alarums and excursions and there were quite a lot of people who had to be spoken to quite firmly from time to time, but by and large we succeeeded beyond all expectations. If anyone had said at the beginning we could keep it up for so long, I wouldn't have believed them."'

We now have to look at the lessons of the war and possible formulae for solution of the continuing conflict in the South Atlantic. And I think the events of the last few days in relation to fishing in the South Atlantic are further evidence that the United Kingdom Government at the present time is still bent on a non-diplomatic solution to almost anything to do with that region of the world. In this little Belgrano Enquiry booklet there are a number if ideas for possible solutions to the problem which have been listed and on which I would like to make one or two brief comments.

The first lesson of the war for the future is that if ever you can find methods of avoiding conflict, you should exhaust those before you engage yourself in conflict. It was in early June 1982 when the bullets were actually flying in the South Atlantic, that Israel invaded the south of Lebanon. And the U.N. Security Council met and adopted a Resolution which made three basic requirements:

1) the cessation of all hostilities by the parties to the dispute.
2) the withdrawal of Israeli troops from Lebanese soil.
3) renewed negotiations to try and solve whatever the problems were which had caused the invasion in first place.

And the United Kingdom went along with that Resolution and voted in favour in the U.N. Security Council. And I remember the reports in the British media of Mr Begin, the Israeli Prime Minister at the time, standing up in the Knesset and saying, "If Britain can use bullets to secure its interests in the South Atlantic, then why shouldn't I do exactly the same to secure my interests in the border region of Northern Israel?"

The second lesson from this war, as indeed from all wars for the future, is that once you have committed your military in a definite engagement against your enemy, talking about the problems ceases. And once you have stopped talking to each other then it is in fact very difficult, given the attitude of most politicians in the world, to begin talking again. Because once bullets begin to fly a machismo and a jingoism are allowed to flourish which makes it appear weak for a politician to say that diplomatic movements are better that military. And we have, in the last four years since the war ended, had a classic example of a Government which is simply unwilling to speak seriously to the other side about the basic causes of that conflict. I would go along fully with David Steel when on more than one occasion he, and indeed increasing numbers of others, has pointed out that it is amazing that we can actually sell weapons and have diplomatic relations with a military Junta up until the 2nd April 1982 and we're now simply not prepared to talk seriously with a democratically elected government in Argentina.

So lesson three must be that when a government with whom you have a war is replaced by a more reasonable government, your first initiative should be to renew the diplomatic contacts with that new government in order to give fresh impetus to the wish for a non-violent solution.

In looking at possible ways forward for the future we have, as we always have, to go back to the complex problem of sovereignty and I don't want to go over in detail again what we said yesterday morning. But I would just say that if British sovereignty is valid then the Falkland Islanders are indeed British subjects living on British soil, but if those claims to sovereignty are not valid then the Falkland Islanders are British subjects living on non-British soil. And until we have a willingness to get a definitive solution to the question of sovereignty, there will never, never, never be a final solution to the problem of the Falkland Islands and the South Atlantic. And the longer the Government continues to duck any willingness to talk about sovereignty, the more difficult they are making a comprehensive solution to the problem for whichever government inherits the role of having to try to find an end to this tragic story.

I believe that one of the major things that could and possibly should happen, is a willingness to be found by both parties to the dispute to submit the issue to the International Court of Justice and to be bound by the findings of the Court. Sadly I don't think that will happen under any British government and probably not under any Argentine government, because I do not believe in their heart of hearts that either side feels that their claim is so absolutely valid that they have 100% chance of winning in the International Court of Justice.

So if we cannot use the International Court of Justice we have to look at other ways of coping with the situation. The Falkland Islanders as I understand it, almost to a person, would like the status quo to be maintained. That in the long term is patently impossible, Because, if I can put it at its crudest, I do not believe that the 54 million British inhabitants of the United Kingdom who don't live on the Falkland Islands, are going to be willing for ever and a day to continue to fork out the sort of money that the status quo will require for the 1,800 or so British citizens living on the Falkland Islands. So in pure economic terms, let alone any other, I do not believe that the wish for the status quo to be maintained is actually a realistic way forward, nor do I believe that it would ever be acceptable to Argentina who will continue, in one way or another, to put pinpricks into the whole problem of the South Atlantic.

People have talked about establishing a U.N. trusteeship. I think there are political problems to establishing a U.N. trusteeship in the Falkland Islands. And the problem as I see it is basically, that if the U.N. according to its traditional pattern of trusteeship territories, appointed a trusteeship in the South Atlantic, it would in fact invite the British as the current administering power to continue to administer the Falkland Islands on behalf of the U.N. Trusteeship Council. And continuing British administration of the Islands, whether direct or under a U.N. trusteeship arrangement, would I imagine be as unacceptable as the present situation is to the Argentine government. I'm not sure how happy the Islanders would be having a U.N. trusteeship. I suspect it's an issue which has never really been seriously discussed and points on the pros and cons of trusteeship actually discussed with people, who by all accounts, if we are to believe those accounts, really don't want to discuss any options for the future except maintenance of the status quo. But a trusteeship should at least be looked at to see whether some form of perhaps alternative administrative arrangements under a trusteeship arrangement could in fact be taken further forward.

Another idea which has been put forward is that until such time as there is, between the United Kingdom and Argentina, a definitive solution to the problem, the Falkland Islands would become a U.N. territory. This would be creating a precedent in terms of international relations because I'm sure, and correct me if I'm wrong, I'm sure there has never before been a U.N. territory. The idea is that because neither Britain nor Argentina has a fully validated claim to the Islands, they would both be willing to place the administration of the Islands in the hands of the United Nations. And the United Nations, under the guidance of the Secretary-General, would establish a modest secretariat, doubtless an international one, presumably without any British or Argentine members in it, but that would be subject to discussion, who would administer the Islands on behalf of the United Nations until such time as the permanent constitutional status of the Islands was worked out. In order to try to give some form of security against outside interference, military or other, in the Falkland Islands the proposal would, the arguers of this point of view suggest, have to contain a small U.N. peacekeeping contingent who would police the Islands on behalf of the United Nations and who would hopefully, being an international force, act as something of a guardian against an unwarranted military or other interference by either Argentina or presumably the United Kingdom.

Another proposal which traditionally has won a modest level of government support by both Labour and Conservative administrations in the United Kingdom, is some form of transfer of sovereignty to Argentina with a period of lease-back to the United Kingdom. I do believe that lease-back is one of the options we should still be very seriously considering, so that we could guarantee to the present generations of Islanders, if we can make suitable arrangements, that they would remain under British administration, but we could not guarantee that for their great-great-grandchildren and beyond. And that would depend on the United Kingdom not least being willing to admit that its claims to sovereignty are not as absolute as suddenly became apparent on the 2nd April 1982. And I have to say again what I said yesterday morning, that if those claims are as absolute as the Prime Minister and others now assure us they are, would they please put back in the Public Record Office all those documents which have been removed from public scrutiny, so that we can share with them rejoicingly in the belief that this claim is now absolute and totally valid. I fear it is not and never will be.

A final solution could be some form of shared sovereignty as the booklet says, 'of the kind which has kept Andorra autonomous for 500 years'. I think that should be looked at more seriously than has been the case hitherto and I believe that we should be willing in the United Kingdom to find what is essentially a compromise with Argentina. And they must be willing to compromise, in order to get what is a politically acceptable settlement to both parties, to the United Kingdom Government, to the government of Argentina, in full consultation whichever proposals have been put forward, with the Falkland Islanders themselves; but on the clear understanding that unless British sovereignty is a proven and accepted fact in international law, we cannot accept that the Falkland Islanders are necessarily legitimate occupiers of the Islands. Until sovereignty is clear cut they may in fact be de facto and not just de jure inhabitants of that area of land in the South Atlantic. Therefore to continue to duck the issue, as successive governments did between the 1960s and the early 1980s, and increasingly to build up a situation in which somehow the Islanders themselves were given a de facto veto on British policy in a much wider area of Latin America than just the South Atlantic, is something which has to be challenged because it is not democratic in any way unless the Islands are legitimately British.

Michael Harbottle

I would like to simply address myself, following on from yesterday, to three particular aspects. The first is Her Majesty's Government's relationship with the United Nations during the course of the events from the invasion by the Argentines 'til the actual engagement at Carlos Bay on, I think it was the 21st May. Secondly, I just want to, because it was raised by Mr Ogden in his presentation yesterday, I do want to talk about the possibilities that are open to the Security Council and to the United Nations in respect of the Charter and in respect of their reaction to conflict situations that arise. And thirdly, I would like to address myself particularly to that item in the present session about lessons for the future on the subject of a system of contingency planning for peaceful settlement of disputes being set up in the United Nations.

So for the first aspect: as a founding member of the United Nations and as one of the Permanent Members of the Security Council, for the United Kingdom to seek the Security Council's authority in the first place to condemn the action of Argentina, and then from that moment (as Malcolm has indicated from the extracts from the Times book, The Insight Report) to separate itself totally from the United Nations — not to seek or to use the machinery of the United Nations which as a founder member it agreed to support — for them to simply turn their backs on it, I think is an action of incredible deceit and of a total infidelity to the rules and to what they committed themselves to at the time of the setting up of the U.N. and the production of the Charter. And so it was that until virtually the beginning of May, until the 7th May, when Peru's initiative ended, it wasn't really until then that the United Nations, through the Secretary-General, came into play. And even then it was not a matter of returning to the Security Council. It was the development on what had started while the Haig initiative was on, as a personal initiative on the part of the Secretary-General, to use his good offices in order to try and help find a solution to the problem peacefully by constantly working with the British Ambassador to the U.N., Anthony Parsons, and, in the beginning, with Costa Mendez, the Argentinian representative. When the Haig initiative came to an end then the Secretary-General's good office's initiatives continued, despite the fact that we still had a position in which virtually the United Kingdom had brushed the U.N. aside as not being of any value or of any vital necessity in the whole matter of settling the dispute.

And one of the things that hasn't been mentioned, but I think is significant, is that on 11th May, when clearly there was some progress in the efforts of the Secretary-General and these were noticeable, these were being reported, at a very crucial moment in that period, Sir Anthony Parsons was called home for a weekend discussion with the Prime Minister, or he came home. He returned two days later and, as has been described elsewhere, from that moment the initiative of the Secretary-General virtually came to an end and there wasn't anything more that he could do at that time. So I would suggest, and I think that this is an area that really does need very careful assessment, a study of the motivations behind Her Majesty's Government in not only totally ignoring the machinery and the good offices of the Secretary-General, but also apparently taking steps to sabotage the successful conclusions of those good offices.

I think it is also interesting to recognise that on the 26th April the Secretary-General announced that 502 in respect of the withdrawal of troops, from that moment applied to the United Kingdom as well as to the Argentine. If in the first instance the United Kingdom sought and got Resolution 502 through, calling for the withdrawal of the troops of Argentina, then they were equally bound by that 502 following that 26th April statement, to withdraw their own forces from offshore at that time.

Now to turn to the second point on the question of the Security Council and the U.N.'s authority. I quoted from Article 39 which indicated the responsibility of the Security Council with regard to the settlement of international disputes affecting international peace and security. But Article 38 says that:

'The Security Council may, if all the parties to any dispute so request, make recommendations to the parties with a view to a specific settlement of the dispute.'

Now that underlines what I said yesterday and I hope it does clarify to Mr Ogden and others that the U.N. is not an authoritarian body that imposes decisions and requirements on its member states. It is there to be used and can in fact operate, as it has in its peacemaking initiatives and its peacekeeping initiatives, with the consent of, or at the request of the parties concerned. In this particular case the parties concerned did *not* request and ultimately it was because they were in no position at that time to create any third party initiative actually in the Island or in respect of peacemaking or peacekeeping, that the criticism that the U.N. did nothing has arisen. That is to me an overriding factor in U.N. action that we really must recognise. It wasn't the fault of the U.N. that no initiative was taken, it was the fault of the parties concerned.

I now turn to the question of contingency planning, and this, as anybody who knows the workings of the U.N., is an incredibly difficult thing to achieve. Since it has no foreign authority of itself it has to conform, in whatever it does, to the wishes and the recommendations and the resolutions of the member states. For a collective of 160 states, that sort of detailed contingency planning for peacekeeping and peacemaking has to have more than a consensus, it has to have an agreement. And if I may just use the example of the Peacekeepers' Handbook which I referred to yesterday: there was a committee, it was known as the Committee of 33, or the Special Committee on Peacekeeping Operations, which had actually sat for 9 years by, I think it was 1976, when the International Peace Academy, of which I was a member at that time in New York, held a meeting with members of that Committee and suggested to them that what was required was a handbook that would set out the whole procedure for U.N. peacekeeping operations, which could then be used as a guidebook for training and for operations. And after two days' discussion they turned to us and said, "We can't do it. We could never get the agreement of the Committee of 33, or within the U.N., to produce a definitive document like that. Why don't you do it?" And two years later I compiled this for the International Peace Academy, and this book is now used by the U.N. for all its U.N. peacekeeping operations; and as I said yesterday, by up to nearly 100 countries as a training manual for peacekeeping operations when they could be called, not only to serve in U.N. peacekeeping operations but as a guide as to how third party operations could be conducted.

U.N. peacekeeping operations are mounted quickly or for an extended period, dependent on the requirement. The nearest one to that kind of model that I would foresee might be used in the

future in the Falkland Islands as an interim U.N. coverage while
negotiations and development of the solution goes on between the
parties concerned within the framework of the U.N., is the model
that was used in West Irian, which is west Papua New Guinea. It
was scheduled for one year but in fact it was subsequently reduced
to 8 months. The U.N. temporary administration actually left
West Irian on the day that it had originally been planned for it to
do, because in the period of that 8 months the parties concerned,
which were the Netherlands and Indonesia had arrived at the
position where a handover could take place.

And so I would suggest to you that there are opportunities within
the U.N. which could be of great value in the Falkland Islands
situation, but which have to be dependent upon the United
Kingdom and Argentina actually recognising that they have a
period of time to settle the dispute and to work to settle it in that
time.

Eric Ogden

The history of the Falkland Islands, the landings, the exploration,
the settlement before 1833 is varied, interesting, lively, and can
be confusing even for the experts. The interest of European and
South American governments ebbed and flowed almost like the
tide. I believe that the British claims to the discovery, settlement
and sovereignty of the Islands are valid but others are entitled to
their own opinions. Of what there can be no doubt is that a British
settlement, administration and sovereignty was established or
re-established in 1833, was maintained without interruption for
147 years until the invasion and occupation by Argentine forces,
and that administration, sovereignty and government was
recognised by the international community, except from time to
time by the administration of the Argentine. In 1833, at the
beginning of that period of British sovereignty, government and
administration, Spain made no claims to the sovereignty of the
Falklands. The Spanish-American Republic of the Rio Plate did
not claim its independence from Spain until about 12 years after
1833.

Interruption: That is wrong, it was 1816.

Eric Ogden: 1816? I will argue the differences about that, but my
information is 1833. Certainly, I think we can ahgree on this, Spain
did not recognise the administration and the independence of
Argentina until some 30 years after that date. Argentina has
pursued her claims as the inheritor of the Spanish Empire against
not only the Falklands but all her mainland neighbours, and has
done so by annexation and agression as much as by diplomacy.
Argentina bases her claims for the Falklands on that inheritance

from Spain and on the basis of geographical proximity. Now on a large-scale map of the world, the Falklands may seem close to Argentina but Buenos Aires is some 900 miles from Stanley which is as far as London is from Prague. The Argentine claims against the British territories are not only for the Falklands but for South Georgia, the South Sandwich Islands, the South Orkneys and for all of British Antarctic territories. None of those can be called close to Argentina. But at least I think it shows that Argentina recognises the importance both of the Falklands as the gateway to Antarctica and for the importance of Antarctica itself. I think that is understood better in Argentina that it is often here in this country.

Now Argentina will claim that her settlement in the Falklands was forcefully dispossessed by British forces in 1833. The facts are that the chief officer of that administration, an Argentine administration, had just been murdered by some of his own compatriots and that those compatriots were removed to London and then back to Argentina. But most of the Argentinian settlements remained and continued to prosper. Even if the Argentine version is correct, that it was a forceful dispossession, an act of war etc, then the facts are that more often that not international boundaries through the whole of history have been decided more by force than by diplomacy. Even if the Argentine version of what happened in 1833 is true, it was not against international law as of that time. And if the basis of the Argentine claim is that of forceful dispossession and therefore it must be given back, were that to be written into international law, then I would suggest that Mexico would claim not only Texas and California, but Utah and Nevada and Colorado. We would claim at least the eastern states of the United States and you might even have the Danes back in Buxton. Because that would be the significance of trying to rewrite the political boundaries of the world as they may or may not have been in 1833. That's an unreal world and not one that we live in in 1986.

There's also the fact that whenever Argentine claims to the Falklands have been made or renewed, that has happened essentially for internal domestic reasons, the Peronistas or the Juntas. The invasion of 1982 was triggered, if you like, essentially because of the internal dissent against the Junta. It was a diversion and it was essentially a reaction to internal Argentine matters rather than anything else. Argentina lost the war she began and the consequences have been accepted, at least by some in Argentina. I wish the Argentine democratic government well, but it's no part of my duties or our duties to sacrifice British lives, British interests, to maintain and secure Argentine democracy.

That is their responsibility not ours. And what kind of a democracy is it that has to maintain the same claims as the Junta, cannot unequivocally denounce the use of force, cannot agree even to discuss diplomatic relations, airlinks, trade and conservation, unless Britain agrees to negotiate about sovereignty? Everyone in the Falkland Islands, everyone in Argentina and everyone here ought to know that, when Argentina talks about negotiations about sovereignty, they're talking about negotiations for the transfer of sovereignty in one way only. Rightly or wrongly, Argentina is neither strong enough or wise enough to want to share sovereignty, or to be able to share sovereignty. Any moves by the United Nations, lease-back or any other way would be acceptable to her only as a way of claiming equal rights with British settlers and one way or another obtaining the whole sovereignty of the Falkland Islands.

Certainly the public relations of President Alfonsin have been superb. If I could get Senor Makin and his colleagues to lend their services to the British Foreign Office or to the Falkland Island Government they might in fact begin to fight some of the battles themselves, instead of leaving it to others. The claims and the promises are better presented than they were by the Junta, but they're exactly the same as those made by the Junta and the people in the Falkland Islands remember only too well that the Argentine promises made, and repeated time and time again before the conflict, were broken within days of the invasion.

There was a recent visit of British Parliamentarians to the International Parliamentary Union Conference in Buenos Aires early this month, in October. The Labour members of that delegation were Donald Anderson, George Foulkes, Michael Maguire and Andrew Faulds. Even they became rather worried by the impression that they got from the Argentine delegation who seemed to say, 'All we have to do is wait for a Labour Government and you will give us the Islands'. And they had to spell out quite clearly, that in fact all the Labour Party was committed to was talking about the sovereignty. That ought not to be read as an agreement now to transfer the sovereignty.

For those who say, 'Well it's costing a lot of money, we can no longer afford to defend you.' I would say that that kind of attitude — 'We defended the Falklands but it's cost a lot of money so there has to be an agreement' — is exactly the same in principle as if anyone on this platform were to go downstairs and up the road to a victim of assault or rape or battery and say, 'Look we sent the police and you were rescued and saved, we put a guard on your house, but we can't afford that guard any more. So the best thing we can do is, we're going to pull out and you'd better go and talk to whoever robbed you, assaulted you and make a deal with him. And if you decide to marry him that will get you off our back, but we can't defend you anymore.' Exactly the same principle of what you're saying to the Falkland Islanders is in that situation.

I'll make another point. Everyone here I think, with maybe one or two exceptions, is going to live here in peace and security and safety whatever happens to the Falkland Islands. I think we should be careful before we tell someone else in those situations, what is best for them. I would take it from a Falkland Islander about what they thought. But if we're going to be safe, we should be careful before we become presumptuous, even arrogant, about telling them what is going to be best for them.

From the time of the liberation, the British Government have promised the Islanders that they would have a referendum, and other people have said well maybe the Islanders will think this, or that, or the other. So my Association commissioned Marplan to undertake a postal ballot of every Falkland Island elector, 1,040 out of the 2,000. It was done with complete confidence, complete privacy and 89% responded and 94% of those said they wanted to continue British sovereignty. We found three of the electors who said quite clearly that they wanted Argentine sovereignty, and I took it as a tribute to the integrity of my Association that in British islands people could say what they wanted freely and openly, and they did. And no one in the Islands has tried to find out who they are. I don't know, neither does anybody else.

The security of the Islands has been guaranteed by British forces and the construction of a Mount Pleasant airport. The costs have been great but 90% of that has been spent on British jobs, British services, British equipment, British employment. The figures that were given from the platform stopped at when the costs dropped down to £300 million but it's £200 million this year and it can fall much further. But before the invasion they were in hundreds of thousands rather than millions and the only reason it's costing us anything at all is because the Argentine threat continues. If Argentina would renounce the use of force and her claims, then in fact it would cost us hundreds rather than hundreds of thousands. The economic development of the Island is going firmly ahead controlled by the Islanders. They have the constitution they asked for and are well in control of their own affairs. Land has been bought from the large farms and subdivided because it was a feudal society and that had to be changed. More and more land is offered from the large farmers than can be handled by the Falkland Island government. The British Government has at long last ended its futile efforts to secure Argentine partnership in the fishing regimes and that offer is still open. If Argentina wants to share in the conservation of the waters of the Southwest Atlantic then that offer is available to them. There have been cries of anguish from some, 'Of course it's going to lead to another war.' When the Russian Foreign Minister was here in July he gave an assurance to the British Foreign Secretary that they weren't going to have any problems with the Russians. The Spanish have said that they're not going to trade, they're not going to observe the rules, but the Spanish Government is different from the Spanish fleet, doesn't in fact own any trawlers in those waters. The Japanese and the Taiwanese and the Koreans will say, 'Don't worry about the policing, we'll do our own policing.' That's the international experience as it goes along.

The Falkland Islanders contrary to some suggestions never were a drain on the British tax payer, and equally the Falkland Islands were never so dependent on communications or trade or hospitals or schools in Argentina as is sometimes suggested.

The only clouds over the Falklands come from Argentina. And how the Falkland Islanders respond to those worries I think is best expressed by an elected councillor of the Falkland Islands when he addressed the United Nations Committee of 24 on the 21st July last. He, an elected Falkland Island councillor, said to the United Nations Committee of 24 in July:

'This Committee of 24 is the one United Nations Committee above all others which deals with the welfare of peoples not just land. So in that Committee it seems right to concentrate on the people who actually live there and what they want, how they see their future, and not just on the land. We, the Falkland Islanders, have been disappointed to see that every year the Argentine delegation tries to turn the issue into a dispute about land, not people. We've been disappointed to see that they deny us the right of self-determination which they claim for themselves. Self-determination is a right, not a privilege, and no committee of the United Nations can either give or dispose of that right, otherwise it becomes a privilege not a right. We present our petition to pursue our right of self-determination and to make it quite clear that we wish to retain our British sovereignty. Our constitution gives us much more control of our own affairs and allows us to develop our political aspirations to ultimate independence if we so want. The economic and the political development of the Islands are firmly in our own hands. The British Government has been called upon to protect us from abuse. It continues to do so in a way which only those who would wish to abuse us could consider aggressive. We are happy with the economic constitutional progress we are making.

We are happy with our association with the United Kingdom
and we will be happy to inform this Committee if at any other
time we think otherwise.'

The Falklands will be discussed at the United Nations in a few
weeks time. I would hope that the British Government have the
good sense to come up with some positive and imaginative ideas.
I would hope that at some time in the future what is not possible
now will be possible then; that at some time children in the
Falklands and in Argentina will look back, and this might take 20,
50 years and say, 'What was all the fuss about — about sovereignty
and land and who owned what way back in 1833?' I would hope
that as we've learned to live together in Europe, then the peoples
of South America and the Southwest Atlantic could learn to live
together. But that has to come when the peoples of all those areas
have the same rights and recognise the rights of other people in
those areas as well.

John Ferguson: Ian Mikardo said that Francis Pym set off on the
weekend of May 1st/2nd to talk with Alexander Haig and Perez
de Cuellar. I think that I'm right in saying that Tam Dalyell or
somebody, who was speaking here earlier, indicated that Francis
Pym did not have an appointment to see Perez de Cuellar and
that that was actually organised privately, that he didn't explicity
go with an appointment.

Ian Mikardo: No, he didn't have an appointment, he went with
an appointment with Al Haig but hoping to arrange an
appointment when he got there, and he did. And his first action
when he got there was to ask the Ambassador to fix an
appointment with Perez de Cuellar.

John Ferguson: We have a slightly different version. Could we
just clarify this?

Malcolm Harper: I can't quote my sources, it was given to me
off the record, but I have it from a very senior Foreign Office
source that Sir Anthony Parsons, the British Ambassador to the
United Nations, had himself to take the initiative to invite Francis
Pym to dinner in his flat in New York on Sunday evening 2nd
May, and he, Anthony Parsons, then invited the U.N. Secretary
General to come to dinner on the same evening. Because there
was no other way in which he could see them being brought
together for a meeting. Because Francis Pym simply did not have
Perez de Cuellar on the list of contacts to make during his visit to
the United States.

Ian Mikardo: Well what was clear was that Francis Pym declined
a meeting in the afternoon. He had a meeting in the morning with
Al Haig, and declined a meeting in the afternoon, because he said
he had to go off to Washington to see Perez de Cuellar. That

much is quite clear. The Ambassador went to the afternoon meeting instead of him.

John Ferguson: I've a question for John Madeley. John Madeley made out very clearly the fact that there was difference of treatment on the part of the British Government of the inhabitants of Diego Garcia and of the Falkland Islanders. One's been aware of this for some time. The suggestion is that there was a change in policy in early March or mid-March 1982 and suggested to Diego Garcians this might have been due to an anticipation of the Falkland Islands conflict. Now I think this is quite an important point, I suppose it's bound to be all speculation, but are we saying that early in March the British Government knew that the conflict over the Falklands was coming?

John Madeley: As you say, this is always speculation and we won't know for many years, if at all. But there was certainly a quite dramatic change of policy. For 17 years the British Government had dragged its heels over giving any kind of decent compensation and very suddenly it did change in early March. And I would guess that amongst all the possibilities it was then considering when it looked at the Falklands in some detail, at least someone in the Foreign Office spotted the contradiction between the way that the Falkland Islanders and the people of Diego Garcia were being treated, and said, 'We really ought to clear this matter up. There's only a couple of million pounds at stake. Let's get it over with.' And that that point was accepted. But that's only a guess.

Joan Hymans: A lot of us were very concerned about the fact that most of the Labour Party Members of the House supported the war. They had, of course, been for years concerned about self-determination in lieu of colonial freedom and in freeing the colonies into independence. Perhaps Ian Mikardo could say whether there was a real understanding of the background to this conflict and the problems of sovereignty.

Ian Mikardo: Well it's impossible to answer for all the members of the Parliamentary Labour Party at that time and to know how far each of them was informed about and understood the background. I recall, going back 30 years, the outrage of the Suez conflict. There is a tendency on such occasions for people to react straight off the top of their heads and start thinking afterwards. And I think it's probably for that reason that in the first flush, when we had our first vote, there were only a relatively small number, a minority of members of the Parliamentary Labour Party, who voted against the Government on this issue. I think if there'd been another vote some time afterwards the result would have been very different because people would then have had time to study and to learn, instead of reacting off the top of their heads. I was one of the minority who voted against and I'm richer on that account because one of the Alliance MPs described us all as traitors and has had to pay us all some damages for it!

Dr G A Makin: Tam Dalyell went to Lima in October 1983. I was with him, and one of the interesting things was that the then Prime Minister of Peru at the time of the conflict, not at the time of our visit, Dr Manuel Ulloa, told us that as Prime Minister he had a number of contacts that he couldn't reveal to us at the time; that they'd told him that the conversations were serious and that the Secretary of State of the United States had good contacts with the U.K. Government. The only name in particular he gave us was Hugh Thomas. He had had several conversations in the course of the month of April and late May, as you know after the sinking of the Sheffield there was another Peruvian initiative. It was Hugh Thomas who was involved. I don't remember informing your committee of this and I wondered whether Mr Dalyell has, because it seems to me that there are more indications that Lord Thomas's involvement is rather more important than we were led to believe.

Ian Mikardo: Well Tam's the only man who could answer that question with authority. But the impression I got was that he was disappointed in his visit to Peru, he had hoped to get a lot more and a lot franker information from the Peruvian Government. For whatever reasons, and inter-governmental relationships are funny things, the Peruvian Government hasn't been very forthcoming in providing information or answering questions, even after the change of government in that country. Nevertheless I rather fancy that it will not be very long before we shall start getting a good deal more information and perhaps some that will throw a vastly different light on what we know and on what we now think.

Nick Kollerstrom: We gather that the Peruvian Government did have documents which showed beyond doubt that the Government's statement that it had not heard about these plans until after sinking the Belgrano was mistaken; and we gathered they would be prepared to release the documents if asked by the Parliamentary Labour Party and not just by anyone else. Could you tell us why the Party has not been prepared to ask the Peruvian Government for these documents?

Ian Mikardo: No, I don't know the answer to that question.

Nick Kollerstrom: What we gathered was that they'd only be prepared to do this if asked by the Labour Party.

Ian Mikardo: You know, the Government has made it clear it's not going to tell and there's not much point in asking — it's a pretty frustrating exercise. We asked too. And there will be no change in that situation unless and until, one or both of two things happen; a change of Government in which we shall be able to get, not all, but some of the information, and a change of view, as I said in answer to the last question, by the Peruvian Government on the amount they are prepared to disclose.

Bill Hetherington: The difference in the way that the Diego Garcians were treated and the way the Falkland Islanders were treated, was this an example of militarism and not racism pure and simple? I would like to question whether it goes deeper than that, that in fact Diego Garcia was an example of both racism and militarism, that both are two sides of the same coin. What I mean by that is that to be racist we could say that a group of people because of their colour, or whatever, are to be treated as less than yourself, if not less than human. And what militarism says is that people who want independence are to be treated as less than yourself, or if necessary less than human, to the point in fact of course, as we saw, that 1,000 people in the Falkland Islands conflict are to be totally wiped off the face of the earth. So the two are equal and it is highly likely that the reason why the Diego Garcians were deprived of their homeland was that. So that you can't look at one side without looking at the other.

John Madeley: Yes I agree with that. There is certainly a suspicion at the very least of racism in this whole affair and you're absolutely right, there is also the military factor. Diego Garcia as I mentioned is an ideal place, or is considered ideal by the Pentagon, to monitor the activities of the Soviet Navy. It's right in the heart of the Indian Ocean, and they wanted it for a support facility, a base as it has now become. And they could get away with it because they felt that Britain could move those people, and Britain was able to. Had the Falkland Islanders been there I doubt if they would.

Helen Trask: One of the conditions for the Ilois to receive their very meagre compensation in 1979 was that they should abandon all rights ever to return to Chagos. Our British Government demanded that they abandon their right to their own home. It's important to recognise that this happened during a Labour Government so that you need to breathe down the necks of all the Parties to find out what is happening. As John said, this was the case for a military facility, now by far and away the biggest American base on British soil. According to figures I have received, in the past three years America has spent $160 million on Diego Garcia for military construction, compared with $306 million on American bases in Britain for military construction. So a third of American expenditure on military construction on American bases on British soil is going on Diego Garcia.

VIII

Conclusions

Dr G. A. Makin

The Peruvian Peace Initiatives involved Argentina, Peru, the United Kingdom and the U.S.A. The Peruvian version of events remains largely unexplored. Early in May 1984 I was in New York at the same time as the Foreign Affairs Committee of the House of Commons interviewed the then Peruvian Permanent Representative to the U.N., Dr Javier Arias Stella, who had been Peru's Minister for Foreign Affairs during the conflict. I had a long talk with him and I must say that it appeared in content to have been held with another person instead of with this Peruvian representative, if I am to go by the way it was reported by Sir Anthony Kershaw in the press conference when the report was published. So in the course of this talk, Arias Stella revealed that the Peruvian Ministry of Foreign Affairs had drawn up a memorandum summarizing the several telephone conversations and meetings in Lima relating to the initiative and that this summary proved to his mind that the British Government knew of the plan by the midday of Saturday May 1st, when he called both the Argentine and the British Ambassadors to his office to inform, on President Belaunde's instructions, of the state of the negotiations involving Alexander Haig as a go-between with the British Government.

Arias Stella stressed that far from the 'mere outline' that Francis Pym has dismissed with typical British haughtiness, even at that early stage, what later came to be known as the 7 points, were then explained consecutively to both Ambassadors.

Arias Stella told me that the best way of securing access to these documents was to contact a career diplomat in Lima, Mr Hubert Wieland, then one of the highest civil servants in that ministry, and at this moment Vice-Minister for Foreign Affairs under President Alan Garcia.

Time went by and personal inquiries led nowhere. Having travelled to Lima with Tam Dalyell to establish whether these documents existed, I had improved my contacts in Lima slightly and tried to get them to verify whether the documents were around, that they weren't a myth.

One of these contacts, Jose Rodriguez Elizondo, then the Foreign News Editor of the weekly *Caretas* spoke to Wieland who confirmed that the documents did exist and that 'they should be officially requested by the Labour Party'. This refers to the point earlier on taken up with you Mr Mikardo. The son of the proprietor of the Peruvian daily *El Commercio*, Alejandro Miro Quesada (Jr) reportedly made the same check and came back to me with the same answer concerning the existence of the documents. A few days later Tam Dalyell 'phoned Hubert Wieland to his office in Lima and, in perfect English, he was assured that the Peruvian papers detailing the timings of conversations and their content did exist. He suggested that a letter might help secure copies. The letter was sent, it hasn't been answered.

If the Peruvian evidence is around, and since the Foreign Affairs Committee was aware of my exchanges with Arias Stella, given my letters to them and a letter published in *The Guardian* late in 1984, why was no effort made to secure these papers? This I must add, is a question aimed primarily at the Foreign Affairs Committee as well as to my colleagues in the British media in general.

Are we sufficiently aware, has it been sufficiently thought through that Clive Ponting did not have access, on his own admission, to the Foreign Office papers relating to the Peruvian initiative, even though he tells me he repeatedly requested them?

Is it not intriguing that a Foreign Office official who must remain unnamed, told one of the researchers of the famed Panorama programme on the Belgrano that the FCO had masses of damning evidence?

Why do the Peruvians refrain from publishing information? That I can answer. Not for the first time former President Fernando Belaunde Terry recently explained in an interview with a journalist in Peru, Fernando Flores Araoz in another respected Peruvian weekly, *Oiga*, published on the 27th October 1986. I quote former President Belaunde Terry's words:

> 'I do not want to say all I know because I intend to promote harmony. After the conflict there was a lot of internal politicking, especially in England, both against and in favour of Mrs Thatcher and I have no wish to become involved in that...'

This is on pages 46 and 47 of my translation.

The same interview reports that Belaunde displayed 'six large volumes'. Belaunde is quoted as having said:

> 'Regarding the talks, we were in touch and I can prove it with several documents which are in my possession.'

There are furthermore in this article two photographs of Belaunde with the papers in his house in Lima.

The journalist was not allowed any more access to the documents that we were when we interviewed the then President in Lima when he was in office in 1983; but the following two points are made by Belaunde in *Oiga's* interview; firstly, the content of the initiative which confirms largely what was published in Gavshon's and Desmond Rice's book:

> 'In addition to a truce, the Peruvian initiative consisted of a withdrawal and a handing over of the administration of the Islands to an international committee manned by representatives of countries acceptable to both parties in conflict. Given a date it was possible to reach a final agreement.' (Page 46)

The date was by the way the 31st December 1982.

But to my mind the most important revelation that appears in this interview is the following one which concerns an Argentine, apparently oral agreement and a British, but written acceptance of the Peruvian Peace Initiative, and this is the first time we hear of it:

> 'The truth of the matter is that Belaunde's proposal came to be accepted by the Argentines. And on the 2nd May, the same day the Belgrano was sunk, the British Ambassador in Lima, Charles Wallace, gave Belaunde his country's written confirmation agreeing to the peace plan. Haig had been in charge of convincing the British.' (*Oiga* article, Page 46)

For the record, Nicanor Costa Mendez — who isn't the most agreeable of persons, or the most credible — informed me as the Junta's Foreign Minister at the time of the conflict, that the Peruvian plan had been accepted in principle by the military and this decision was communicated to the Peruvians in the understanding that it was being relayed to the British Foreign Secretary. The reason, he held, for this acceptance was that the Haig initiatives allowed the British to retain possession of the Islands as it was envisaged that they would be under British administration. This was unacceptable, according to Costa Mendez, as there was then no guarantee that there would ever be any substantive progress. The Peruvian plan was different in this crucial aspect, holds Cost Mendez.

All this British searching into the past may not be mere internal politics if it erodes the reputation and resolve of the main obstacle to a negotiated compromise that, according to a number of public opinion surveys, would be acceptable to British and Argentine public opinion. Should my motives as an Argentine in this whole matter be of any consequence, let me briefly and lastly say that I sought to aid this erosion of an impediment.

The Malvinas issue is important in Argentina and in terms of Argentine democracy because the Argentine nation, as Egypt, as Panama, as China, feels defiled by the past and the present situation. Should democracy, which is very healthy for internal reasons, add a negotiated settlement to its achievements, I believe I may have made a small contribution towards consolidating a democracy in my country. I also believe that territorial aggrandizement is far from the thoughts of President Alfonsin and his supporters.

As to what would be acceptable to the Argentine body politic, given my talks with the Radicals and the Peronists, I believe that a short lease-back (25 years given the Panama and the Hong Kong precedents), coupled with international guarantees for the Islanders, concerning their language, their right to retain British nationality, internal democracy, common law, their own educational system, health care etc., and Islander autonomy along with even further compromises towards joint and international exploitation of the other islands and the Antarctic sector would form a package that would be acceptable, once negotiations began of course, with no restrictions as urged by *The Financial Times* and *The Economist* this week. Argentina is not, I submit, obsessed by sovereignty as Sir Geoffrey Howe holds. It has been through British prevarications between 1966 and 1982 documented in the Franks report, that could have been written by an Argentine, that the reasons for Argentine behaviour arise. Britain has a credibility problem in as much as sovereignty, the core of the dispute between both our countries, continues to be excluded and, until this situation is resolved, the conflict in its present dangerous form will, I fear, simmer on. The latest moves by the U.K. Government will only make things 'fishier'.

Clive Ponting

I would like to start, because it was where I got involved in this whole saga, with the fact that there has been a consistent and deliberate cover-up by the British Government of the facts surrounding the sinking of the Belgrano, for two years. Now whatever one might think about the standards of the British Government, it is unusual, to say the least, to see it sustain in such a deliberate way, a series of deliberately misleading and incorrect statements and refusals to answer questions and so on. Now I think you've got to ask yourself, why was the Government doing it? At the moment, nobody's managed to get to the bottom of what it is. I think there are probably two explanations, which are not mutually exclusive. In fact they may well both be true. There's the whole Peruvian aspect as Willy has already stated. The other is that the British Government themselves actually thought that the sinking of the Belgrano was, if not illegal, so near to it in International Law and had put them in such an embarrassing position with international public opinion, that they had to conceal the real reasons for their actions. And that their whole strategy of trying to show that all their actions during the Falklands war were immediate reactions to deliberate Argentine provocation, was not in fact true. And the sort of evidence that we were discussing yesterday shows that the British Government at the time, and the Foreign Secretary and the Attorney-General, believed that the actions that were being taken at the end of April and the beginning of May 1982 were not in fact legal in International Law.

These questions have been around now for four years and have never yet been properly answered or investigated. I think this comes back to one of the crucial problems in Britain and that is the accountability of government: because British government is not really accountable to anybody in the last resort. The problem is that in the House of Commons it controls the majority; and unlike, say, the American Senate, the M.P.s of the majority Party, in the last resort when the pressure is on, will vote to support the Government. They don't have their own independent power base that they can use to criticise the Government. The Select Committee system is also designed in the last resort to back up the Government, because the Government M.P.s have a majority on every Select Committee. And as Ian Mikardo found during the Foreign Affairs Committee investigation of the Belgrano sinking, obviously for public opinion they had to go through the motions of conducting an inquiry, but every time they got to the crucial issues and were asking the crucial questions the Tory majority voted not to ask the questions, or not to seek further evidence. Now under the British system there is no way you can get round this.

What other methods are open if we are to take the issue any further? The Select Committee has obviously reached the end of the road. I mean not only was the Majority Report virtually a whitewash of the Government's actions but the dissenting Minority Report by the Labour Party members has been ignored and not even debated in the House of Commons. We could I suppose have a committee of Privy Councillors to investigate it but I don't believe that the Franks Committee Report would give us much confidence in the outcome of the establishment looking yet again at the actions of the establishment during the sinking of the Belgrano.

The only other possibility would be the setting up of a Tribunal of Inquiry taking evidence under oath under the 1921 Act. But again to set it up there has to be a majority vote of both Houses of Parliament and obviously under the current Government there will not be such a vote.

And so we're left in the end with the fact that the Government, if it chooses not to be accountable or finds difficulties, can always find ways round problems and not be accountable either to Parliament or public opinion. And if, as Willy is saying, documents exist inside the Foreign Office as they may well do, they are known to a number of civil servants, but they're placed in an extremely difficult position of knowing what to do about it, even if they know the Government is still lying about the Peruvian Peace Plan. And so we're left with this whole situation I think, where British Government in a crisis is left unaccountable, where we don't have the American system as was shown in Watergate where people were prepared to actually take on the Government. We don't have much of an independent legal system in this country either, except in the last resort as I was lucky enough to discover.

So I think we are left with this overriding question, not only have we not yet got to the bottom of what's at the sinking of the Belgrano, but we haven't yet got to the bottom of the problem of how you make British Government accountable both to Parliament and the public at the same time.

Ian Mikardo

I've one or two points to make about what might be described as 'Where do we go from here as far as the Falklands are concerned?' But before I do, I want to comment on two of the things that have been said before me. First to answer William's question, why didn't the Foreign Affairs Committee ask for the Peruvian papers? I would have thought the answer to that question is so obvious that it isn't worth asking. The Foreign Affairs Committee didn't ask for the papers for the same reason that they didn't ask the 30 questions of the Government that we thought should be asked: because there is a Conservative majority who saw the dangers to the Government of the truth coming out. The Labour Minority on that Committee did ask, as I said earlier, not only directly but through some intermediaries as well. We very quickly were given to understand what William has just spelled out for us — namely, that the government of Belaunde Terry was determined that it wouldn't get involved in, or even be used in, a purely British civil war between the British Government and its opposition in the House of Commons. There was nothing in it for them as they saw. I must say I was a bit surprised after the change of government in Peru that the incoming government didn't take a somewhat different point of view. It looks, from what William has told us and what he has said in the note he's distributed, that happily they are beginning to take such a different view and that even if indirectly, they will make some information available which wasn't. But certainly that is new, and we got the brush off when we tried. After the change of government in Peru a senior member of another Latin American Government which was very close to Alan Garcia volunteered to act as an intermediary to try and get the papers and he got nowhere either.

Now with great respect I must differ from Clive in his contention that the departmental Select Committees are a part of the instruments of government, a part of the ways in which government can manipulate the House of Commons. It's not true. Most of the time a minority on a Select Committee has got to make a stark choice between trying to get some bits in that are along the lines of its own thinking, or having a confrontation as we did in the case of the Belgrano, and producing a separate report. But of course it's not true even of our own Foreign Affairs Committee with its 7 to 4 Conservative majority and a chairman who is beginning to come increasingly in line with Foreign Office thinking much more than he was. It isn't true even of our own Committee that we've been a tool of Government. We condemn the Government roundly and unanimously for its inadequate response to the famine in Africa. We condemn the Government roundly for its idiotic decision to withdraw Great Britain from UNESCO and we are reopening that inquiry now, and that was unanimous too. We said some things in our report on South Africa, on the consequences of sanctions in South Africa which the Government has disliked very violently indeed. We didn't say all the things that we on the Labour side would have liked, and of course the Government is in very hot water over its attitude to the Select Committee Inquiry on the Westland Affair, and in hot water not only from the opposition but from some of its own members as well.

I quoted from one of the three inquiries the Select Committee has done on the Falkland Islands. I quoted from the one about the events surrounding the weekend of 1st/2nd May 1982. We also did a report on, to use the phrase I used a little while ago, 'Where do we go from here about the Falklands?' And out of that I want to make three points.

The first is about the Falkland Islanders' veto. We made it quite clear in that report that we consider the concept of a veto for ever, or a veto for any extended length of time whatever, to be a nonsense. And of course if you think about it for a moment it is a nonsense. I have no doubt we could take a referendum in the

London Borough of Tower Hamlets and we would get 99.2% of those who vote being opposed to the rate-capping of the Borough Council, but the Government thinks that the question of whether some boroughs should be rate-capped is a matter which is a part of national policy to be decided nationally. Successive Governments, dealing with the problems of Northern Ireland, have changed their policies from time to time about Northern Ireland but at no time have they said that the one and half million, not 1,800, one and half million people in Northern Ireland have the right to tell a British Government what to do about Northern Ireland or to veto any policies or actions of a British Government. When I was a member of a study group in Northern Ireland I went to a border village which coincidentally has a population of 1,800, and they told me they could get an overwhelming majority in favour of the boundary being shifted, the border being shifted slightly in order to put them into the Republic. But I do not believe that any British Government would have acceded to that.

The second of these three points is about the cost. Eric Ogden was a bit glib about that I must say. In our Report we showed that it costs almost precisely 1,000 times as much to defend each Falkland Islander as it does to defend each inhabitant of this island. In round terms it costs about £250 a year to defend each of the people in this room. It costs about £250,000 a year to defend each Falkland Islander man, woman or child. And therefore one of my colleagues on the platform who said a little while ago that the 55 million tax payers, or people of this country — how ever many of them are tax payers — are not for ever going to stand for that, was stating no more than what must be self-evident truth.

The third point is about the recently applied fishing limitation zone. We looked at that very carefully in the course of our examination of the future of the Falkland Islands and we looked carefully at what were its economic prospects as well as what was its political future. We had representations from the Islanders who wanted a 200-mile fishing zone, not to protect fish, not to protect against over-fishing, but in order to get revenue from licences. And we examined all this very closely. And we asked the Royal Navy how much it would cost, and they were very chary about putting a figure on it. But they made it abundantly clear that their enthusiasm for the project was a little less than wild, that they didn't fancy much policing or the cost of policing waters at that distance, nor did they think it was a really practical operation. A little bit of arithmetic will work out the number of square miles in that circle with a slight break in it, of 150 mile radius. It's a lot a square miles of water and the Royal Navy didn't think that was an awfully good idea. It's not at all like policing the North Sea or the waters around the northern Scottish islands and anyway it is highly doubtful whether the thing is going to be self-financing. I will make a forecast. I'm always hesitant to prophesy, because I am very conscious of George Elliot's dictum that 'prophecy is the most gratuitous form of error' because people only remember the tips you gave that lose and not the tips you gave that won. So I'm hesitant to prophesy but I will make a prophecy. No single application for a fishing licence will ever be refused, which shows that the maintenance of stocks and protection against over-fishing, is not and will not be the purpose of the exercise.

John Ferguson: I'll put two questions chairman. One is a question to Dr Makin, would he just clarify so that we are absolutely clear what he said. I understand that Charles Wallace gave British written agreement of the Peruvian Peace Plan on that afternoon of May 2nd and that must imply that they had knowledge of the Peace Plan in detail at least 24 hours beforehand if not longer.

Dr G.A. Makin: Precisely. The only difference I have with what you paraphrase shall we say, is the afternoon bit. The quote says 2nd May it doesn't make unfortunately any precision as to time.

John Ferguson: Thank you, that's clarified that. And then I would just like to raise the question, whether in view of the failure of the Foreign Affairs Select Committee, there should be an inquiry, a Tribunal of Inquiry, I think it was Ian Mikardo who commented on that? We have got clearly I think by everybody's agreement, a Select Committee Report which does not go into all the facts which the general public, whom we here represent want to know. Now, we've been given a picture by Clive Ponting that none of these other procedures is going to get any further. Is there any way we could or should advocate which could possibly get at more of the facts than we have before us?

Clive Ponting: If I knew the answer to that question, I mean that is the crucial question! You could have a Tribunal of Inquiry of course, if you had a different Government that had a majority in the House of Commons and could impose it, and if they could get it through the House of Lords as well. Though I wonder whether any other Government would actually dare impose a Tribunal of Inquiry on the actions of a previous Government because I'm not quite sure they'd like to set that sort of precedent for it being done against them later.

Duncan Smith: Might I ask a question as Ian Mikardo is almost the father of Select Committess in the House of Commons? Should Select Committees be authorised to compel ministers and civil servants to give evidence on oath at the request of the Committee as a whole or at the unanimous request of the Opposition Members? Would this be practicable?

Ian Mikardo: Honestly — it's never been put to me before. My first reaction is that the whole system would be changed and not changed for the better if you had evidence given on oath. It would turn the Select Committee into a court and I think it would reduce the incidence of member of Select Committees of different Parties coming to an agreement and especially an agreement on a conclusion not very pleasant for the Government. I think the way we take evidence now is fine. Select Committees have great powers, we can send for persons and papers. As long as anyone is British and not a member of the House of Lords we can subpoena anyone. It isn't actually a subpoena. We can require anyone to come and give evidence to us and to produce papers, though we are always open to requests from them that they should give evidence in private if there is some element of confidentiality, or present papers other than for publication. I think by and large the system works well. You must remember the new group of departmental committees is fairly new. We've only had them three or four years, and they're going to take a bit of time to bed in, and the rows that there have been about Westland and the like, I think will result in the strengthening of the committees and not the weakening. My reaction to the question is I think that the proposal to have evidence under oath could turn us into a court of law. I think you could not deny legal representation to people who were giving evidence on oath and then we become a court and not a committee.

Mrs Harbottle: As Mr Ogden was speaking in Session 7 my mind went back to Cyprus because I was born and brought up and lived all my life in Cyprus, and I remember very well how dismally we thought of the possibility of Cyprus not being British anymore. And it becomes a psychological obsession that you simply cannot accept the idea of change. And I would like to know from Mr Ogden what kind of reciprocal arrangements exist already among the Islanders? Do they for example go there to secondary school, to University? Do they go there with difficult cases when they are expecting babies? What is that kind of rapprochement between these two countries? Because if it exists already it's something to be built upon. And I agree very much with that comment in the little booklet that we need to understand how to use the United Nations more, because the United Nations is full of examples of how you can collaborate but because you're so jolly ignorant about it we don't accept that this is a possibility. And I wondered whether this could be looked into because it's a very deep psychological problem as well.

Diana Gould: I'm, going to try to reply to your questions. Mr Eric Ogden did give his apologies but he did have to get away.

What has been going on to try to help the Islanders really to
come to terms with any future developments? I think Eric Ogden
dismissed this out of hand today. He said that he wouldn't say
there was a lot of help with education, hospitals etc. Well I'm
afraid that isn't true because there was the Communications
Agreement, which I believe was in the early 1970s. It was set up
in order to try to help the Islanders get used to the Argentinian
presence and their ways. The Communications Agreement for
instance meant that they took over all the air communications.
They built an airstrip and there were regular routes in and out
from the Falklands to the Argentine. They also supplied all the
fuel to the Island. The airfield and the fuel terminal were actually
staffed by Argentinians and had been staffed by Argentinians for
all those years, and so they were used to having Argentinians living
on their Islands. Because of the air routes, there was quite a tourist
trade in the Falklands with people from the Argentine coming
over to see the Islands.

In case of serious illnesses patients used to go to hospital in
Buenos Aires. Now they come to Wroughton RAF hospital 8,000
miles from their home. I know of at least two cases of people who
have died there, Falkland Islanders, 8,000 miles away from their
relatives.

Secondary education was provided by Argentina and this was a
further consequence of the Communications Agreement.

Dr G.A. Makin: I just wanted to add a little to what Diana has
said. 21% of Islander trade went through Argentina between 1972
and 1982. This is something that of course the Islanders deny.
There was a scheme whereby the school children of secondary age
went to school in Argentina — and they did not go to any ordinary
school. They went to the most expensive schools in Argentina so
that they could receive further education in Britain, and that meant
fees of several thousand pounds a year in each case. And that was
quite a considerable outlay since we were not paying the same
amount for our own citizens. So the Islanders received a privilege
for which they have not been grateful. 25 Islanders a year went
to receive this expensive education in Argentina. One of the
families were the sons of Mr Peter Luga who recently created such
a fuss about the trip by the Argentine pilot's family, even reaching
the point of insinuating that they were spies. If you read the
appendices to the Minutes of evidence of the first Falkland Islands
Enquiry of the Foreign Affairs Committee you will read such
choice quotes as:

'Argentines, as a consequence of their being Latin, are by
their very nature violent.'

I would therefore conclude that trying to come to an arrangement with such a population is extremely difficult if not impossible. Other means have to be used.

Ian MacPhail: There is missing from our discussion of this unhappy political charade one powerful name, and that is the name of Lord Carrington which hasn't been mentioned at all. I remember some three months after the war being with Charles Orliz from Lima, because I have interests in Peru, and Charles reflecting on the war, presented the interesting view that perhaps the most serious casualty of the war was Lord Carrington. Does the panel have any views about his part in this?

Malcolm Harper: Well I speak in an entirely personal capacity. I think Lord Carrington was probably the best Foreign Secretary we've had in 15 or more years and I think that in domestic United Kingdom political terms the acceptance of his resignation by Mrs Thatcher in April 1982 was a disaster. Lord Carrington, since he became Foreign Secretary in 1979, had been a party to one or two highly significant acts of diplomacy and I think in particular of the Lancaster House negotiations which led to the independence of Zimbabwe. And I remember particularly when there was to be a Commonwealth Prime Ministers' Heads of Government conference in Zambia, and the issue of Zimbabwean independence was raging, the 'Times of Zambia' and elsewhere were raging against the British Prime Minister who they feared was going to sell out to Ian Smith. And by the end of the conference in Lusaka there had been a very decisive, we're not allowed to call them U turns, but there'd been some sort of turn by the head of the British Government in terms of independence for Zimbabwe. And I have a lot of circumstantial, but I think accurate, evidence to suggest that that was the influence of Peter Carrington as British Foreign Secretary. So I would share with you a feeling both at the time and since, and that's no criticism of his successors, but by accepting that resignation the Prime Minister actually lost one of the ablest Foreign Secretaries we've had for a very long time.

Ian Mikardo: I'd like to add a word to that. The questioner might like to read paragraphs 4 to 8 of Section 2 of the Minority Report of the Foreign Affairs Committee, in which we record the warnings continuously given by Lord Carrington about the problems surrounding the Falklands from 1979 onwards, and particularly about his objection to the withdrawal of Endurance. It seems almost incredible that Carrington wrote to John Nott three times to ask to have a talk with him about the withdrawal of Endurance, and never even got a reply.

Clive Ponting: I think there was one other honourable member in the Foreign Office of all that team that resigned at the beginning of the war and actually that was Humphrey Atkins. What happened to him was, on the day of the actual invasion itself he made a statement in the House of Commons that turned out to be slightly wrong, about the exact time they'd last been in contact with Port Stanley, only by an hour and a half. Yet the next day at the beginning of the Emergency Debate on the Saturday he made a personal statement to the House explaining how he'd misled them and apologising — the last minister to actually do that over the Falklands, and a very different approach to the consistent cover-up afterwards.

Ian MacPhail: I think the point is that obviously the wrong people resigned. The reason for my raising this is not a criticism of this admirable Enquiry but because the report that people have given will become an historical document in the years that follow and not to mention anything in it all of Lord Carrington, and I don't want to embrace his political views in any way whatsoever, would be an error.

Ian Mikardo: Well of course it is very common that it is the wrong people who resign, because the people who resign are the honourable ones. The crooks stay on.

Bill Hetherington: This is a question for William Makin. The quarrel about the Falkland Islands from the Argentine point of view goes back to William's ancestors and his compatriot's ancestors for several generations back to 1833. And it's a quarrel with the ancestors of the present Islanders. And I ask him to think about for how long one ancestor's quarrels have to be perpetuated as your own quarrels? There was a period, several centuries in fact, for which the British Crown pursued a claim on the sovereignty of France, and the official title of the King was the King of Great Britain, France and Ireland which was then dropped when France became revolutionary and George III didn't want to know them anymore. But it was a ridiculous claim that British people have now entirely forgotten about. Can there ever be a time when the Argentines can say, 'Here is a group of people who are definitely different from us, culturally different from us, they speak a different language, they live in a self-contained island. We will leave them alone, we will trade with them, but we won't lay claim to them any more?' And that doesn't mean to say I want British claim either. I think that is essentially the bottom line of treating other people, living your own life without interference from anybody and the word sovereignty wouldn't enter into it.

Dr G.A. Makin: Yes, to begin from the end I think it's a very good idea and I've discussed this several times with several M.P.s that the word sovereignty is a concept that should be dismembered. We can talk about political authority, judicial jurisdiction, educational system, form-filling, languages etc etc.

So that is something that can be usefully dismembered and I know politicians in Britain and in Argentina thinking along those lines. Now I'm going to generalise very dangerously about the past. But each Nation State, and I speak more as a political scientist than as a journalist, has its own version of its past. And Britain always much too virtuously espouses the forgetting of somebody else's past and a bit of the British past that they don't want to remember. Britain occupied the Islands in 1833 at a period at which Argentina was weak, just as they defeated Argentina in 1982 when it was weak. And this is not something Britain can legislate that Argentines should forget. In due time it might be forgotten and Argentina will agree to a compromise, but as an expert in Argentine politics I can't see any political animal in Argentina resigning the Argentine claim. It would be unreal to inform you that that is possible.

Bill Hetherington: What you're saying is that it is built into the concept of the Nation State and the great majority of the Argentinian people feel that this argument of 150 years ago still has to be pursued now.

Dr G.A. Makin: Yes.

Bill Hetherington: Regardless of the fact that presumably no individual Argentinian feels that he is personally involved... I'm sure they can't feel that?

Dr G.A. Makin: Yes they do because you see the Islanders, in as much as they were intransigent in 1980, did prevent a compromise from taking place. So I cannot fully accept, although I would for the sake of political expediency and for a compromise, eventually accept, but I cannot for the time being accept and I don't think most Argentines could accept, that the Falkland Islanders have no quarrel with Argentina. The kind, and I meet several Falkland Islanders, the kind of insult that is levelled at Argentina from the Falkland Islanders, you have had two instances of from Mr Ogden who is not an Islander. But you must believe me that it is exceedingly violent. So it is very difficult to postulate that such a thing should be forgotten. It's unfortunately impractical I'm afraid.

Michael Harbottle: There are two question that are posed in the Handbook. One is the question of self-defence and that's referred to twice. And the first instance is whether the use of self-defence as a justification of the sinking of the Belgrano provided a precedent which was used by President Reagan in defending the raid on Libya. I think the answer must be no because it's not within the same circumstances. It wasn't basically against the people who carried out the 'aggression' against the United States and I think it would be very difficult for anybody to suggest that this was a self-defence factor, particularly as it was not directed against the people who'd carried out the terrorist act against them.

The other point about whether the International Court of Justice should provide a definition of self-defence which all nations should be urged to accept: there is a very definite difficulty here, for instance you might remember that United Nations took, I think, 24 years to come up with a definition of aggression and they still haven't worked out a definition of terrorism. And so if we go into this highly controversial area to get a definition of self-defence, I don't think that we would see one, even if it would be acceptable, before the end of this century.

The last question referred to the Resolution that the General Assembly passed in their last session. Obviously one would hope to see that the implementation of that Resolution and the negotiations and discussions for it to be achieved, should in fact go ahead and should start now and continue until such a time as agreement is reached. But it does strike me that in fact at this point in time that it is the United Kingdom that is in default of the Security Council's Resolution 502 which called for the withdrawal of *all* troops. Whatever way it was done, the Argentine troops are not actually at this moment in the Falkland Islands, the British troops are. If that negotiation is to be effective then there has to be a definite stage of withdrawal of British troops from the Falkland Islands because it creates part of the problem of arriving at a solution.

Diana Gould: Following on Brigadier Michael Harbottle's point concerning the precedent which has been created: the excuse that the Government gave and repeated in its White Paper, was that the Belgrano was a threat to the mission of our forces in the South Atlantic. If the warning of the 23rd April was valid and covered a threat to the *mission*, what was the greatest threat to the *mission* of our forces? That was, as we all know, the landbased aircraft with their Exocets. That warning of the 23rd was able to cover, if it covered the sinking of the Belgrano, an attack on the mainland airfields. This was creating a precedent which could be used in future by countries taking the law into their own hands and saying, 'Well it was a threat to the mission,' so that they could go in to another country. I said this back in January long before the Libyan raid.

One last point: we have given the Falkland Islanders rights which none of us possess, nobody in this room, nobody in this country possesses, and that is the right to live and work in the place of their choice. We do not have that right. Go to any mining village where a mine has closed down because it was uneconomic — those people have no longer the right to work where they wished to work. Ask people who have lived in an area where, for the greater good, it has been decided perhaps that a road has to go through — they have been subjected to compulsory purchase. I think the principle in this country is that you take note of what is right for the greater good for the majority and I think this is what applies in this case. The people of this country are the majority — there are only 1,800 Islanders down there.

Falklands Enquiry
Summary of the Assessors' Findings

The Assessors' main conclusions are as follows:-

1. In spite of a long history showing the passionate belief in her claims to the Falklands by Argentina, and despite clear warnings of the possibility of an attack, the Government failed to take elementary military precautions to protect the islands. Also at no time in 1982, prior to the invasion, was there a clear communication to Argentina that in the event of any attack, Britain would fight to defend the islands.

2. Having obtained the adoption of Resolution 502 in the Security Council, on 2nd. April 1982, condemning Argentina's action and calling for a withdrawal of her forces pending a negotiated settlement, Britain effectively ignored the United Nations.

3. Over the crucial weekend of 1st. and 2nd. May which culminated in the sinking of the Belgrano and virtually scotched any hope of a peaceful settlement, Britain should have been aware of the fact that when the Haig peace shuttle failed on 29th. April, the U.N. Secretary-General was preparing his own plan for a peaceful settlement. Evidence was given to the Enquiry suggesting that the Government had knowledge of the Peruvian Peace Plan before the sinking of the Belgrano. It is important to establish authoritatively whether this is so or not.

4. The Government appeared to have abandoned the stated policy of using minimum force necessary to secure a diplomatic solution well before the first weekend in May, whilst publicly appearing to continue with that policy.

5. The War Cabinet decided to make a major escalation to the hostilities on 30th. April by authorising an attack on the Argentine Carrier, Veinticinco de Mayo, without warning when it was many miles outside the Total Exclusion Zone, which had come into effect only on that day, ignoring the advice of the principal law

officer, the Attorney-General and the Foreign Secretary in so doing. The failure to find the carrier then led on, without any further advice by the special committee of senior officials (the Mandarins' Committee), to the change of Rules of Engagement allowing attacks on any Argentine warship outside the Total Exclusion Zone, and thus to the sinking of the Belgrano on 2nd. May.

6.   No adequate answer has ever been given to the question why the Belgrano was sunk when it had been sailing away from the Falklands for eleven hours, but not attacked when it was sailing towards the islands although sighted and then followed by H.M.S. Conqueror for the previous eighteen hours.

7.   No evidence has been discovered in the five years since the Argentine invasion, in spite of the Ponting Trial and the Foreign Affairs Committee Inquiry, which in any way points to a threat to National Security as a justification for the lengthy continued withholding of official information which might throw light on the sinking of the Belgrano.

8.   The lesson to be learned from the sequence of events which occurred at the beginning of May 1982 is that even what may be by world standards a minor dispute, can easily and dangerously escalate into violent conflict. The implications with regard to a major crisis, involving the possible use of nuclear weapons, are frightening to contemplate.

9.   The Government now has no policy for the islands which makes any political, economic or military sense. Suggestions now, that in order to pay for Trident there will be cuts in the number of Naval surface ships, will affect the number available to patrol the South Atlantic waters, unless this is done to the detriment of our commitments nearer home.

10.   It remains unclear whether the Government was merely guilty of incompetence in failing to protect the islands before the Argentine attack and so involving Britain in an avoidable war, or whether they also deliberatley rejected the possibility of a peaceful outcome, preferring a military solution. The full price of the conflict in the South Atlantic in 1982, financial, military, economic and diplomatic has yet to be paid.

The full Assessors' Report is available from
Diane Gould, Belgrano Action Group, Tel: 0285 4027

APPENDIX I

U.N. Resolution 2065

**As Recommended by Fourth Committee A/6160,
Adopted by Assembly on 16 December 1965
Meeting 1398, By Roll-Call Vote of 90 to 0
With 14 Abstentions, as Follows:**

In favour: Afghanistan, Algeria, Argentina, Austria, Belgium, Bolivia, Brazil, Bulgaria, Burma, Burundi, Belorussian SSR, Cameroun, Central African Republic, Ceylon, Chile, China, Colombia, Congo (Brazzaville), Democratic Republic of the Congo, Cost Rica, Cuba, Czechoslovakia, Dahomey, Dominican Republic, El Salvador, Ethiopia, Gabon, Ghana, Greece, Guatemala, Guinea, Haiti, Honduras, Hungary, India, Iran, Iraq, Ireland, Israel, Italy, Ivory Cost, Jamaica, Japan, Jordan, Kenya, Kuwait, Lebanon, Liberia, Libya, Luxembourg, Madagascar, Malawi, Malaysia, Maldive Islands, Mali, Mauritania, Mexico, Mongolia, Morocco, Nepal, Nicaragua, Niger, Nigeria, Pakistan, Panama, Paraguay, Peru, Philippines, Poland, Romania, Rwanda, Saudi Arabia, Senegal, Sierra Leone, Somalia, Spain, Sudan, Syria, Thailand, Togo, Trinidad and Tobago, Tunisia, Turkey, Uganda, Ukranian SSR, USSR, United Arab Republic, United Republic of Tanzania, Upper Volta, Uruguay, Venezuela, Yemen, Yugoslavia, Zambia.
Against: None.
Abstaining: Australia, Canada, Denmark, Finland, France, Ireland, Netherlands, New Zealand, Norway, Portugal, South Africa, Sweden, United Kingdom, United States.
"The General Assembly,
Having examined the question of the Falkland Islands (Malvinas),

Taking into account the chapters of the reports of the Special Committee on the Situation with regard to the Implementation of the Declaration on the Granting of Independence to Colonial Countries and Peoples relating to the Falkland Islands (Malvinas), and in particular the conclusions adopted by the Committee with reference to that Territory.

Considering that its resolution 1514 (XV) of 14 December 1960 was prompted by the cherished aim of bringing to an end everywhere colonialism in all its forms, one of which covers the case of the Falkland Islands (Malvinas),

Noting the existence of a dispute between the Governments of Argentina and the United Kingdom of Great Britain and Northern Ireland concerning sovereignty over the said Islands,

1. **Invites** the Governments of Argentina and the United Kingdom of Great Britain and Northern Ireland to proceed without delay with the negotiations recommended by the Special Committee on the Situation with regard to the Implementation of the Declaration on the Granting of Independence to Colonial Countries and Peoples with a view to finding a peaceful solution to the problem, bearing in mind the provisions and objectives of the Charter of the United Nations and of General Assembly resolution 1514 (XV) and the interests of the population of the Falkland Islands (Malvinas).

2. **Requests** the two Governments to report to the Special Committee and to the General Assembly at its twenty-first Session on the results of the negotiations."

U.N. Resolution 502 (1982)

Adopted by the Security Council
at its 2350th Meeting, on 3 April 1982

The Security Council,

Recalling the statement made by the President of the Security Council on 1 April 1982 (S/14944) calling on the Governments of Argentina and the United Kingdom of Great Britain and Northern Ireland to refrain from the use of threat of force in the region of the Falkland Islands (Islas Malvinas),

Deeply disturbed at reports of an invasion on 2 April 1982 by armed forces of Argentina,

Determining that there exists a breach of the peace in the region of the Falkland Islands (Islas Malvinas),

1. **Demands** an immediate cessation of hostilities,

2. **Demands** an immediate withdrawal of all Argentine forces from the Falkland Islands (Islas Malvinas),

3. **Calls** on the Governments of Argentina and the United Kingdom to seek a diplomatic solution to their differences and to respect fully the purposes and principles of the Charter of the United Nations.

Summary of the Haig Memorandum of Agreement, 27th April 1982

(based on the full plan given in Appendix 3A Gavshon and Rice:
The Sinking of the Belgrano, **Secker and Warburg 1984)**

1.   Immediate cessation of hostilities.

2.   Simultaneous and mutual withdrawal of forces. U.S. to verify compliance.

3.   Both governments to terminate simultaneously all restrictions adopted in connection with the current controversy.

4.   Both governments and U.S. to each appoint a representative to constitute a Special Interim Authority.

5.   Pending a definitive settlement all decisions by the local administration to be submitted to the Special Interim Authority. The local administration to be enlarged to include representatives of the Argentine Government.

6.   The Special Interim Authority to propose to the two Governments the adoption of appropriate measures on settlement, travel, transportation etc. Such provisions should not prejudice the rights and guarantees heretofore enjoyed by the islanders.

7.   December 31st 1982 will conclude the interim period.

8.   Proposals and recommendations to be made as early as practicable in order to reach a settlement, including the manner of taking into account the wishes and interests of the islanders, the development of the resources of the islands, and possible compensation arrangements.

9.   If it is not possible to conclude the negotiations by December 31, 1982, on request of both Governments, the U.S. would seek to resolve the dispute within 6 months.

10.   The Agreement to enter into force on the date of signature.

Peace Proposals

The Peruvian Peace Plan (According to Gavshon and Rice)

1. Immediate ceasefire.
2. Simultaneous and mutual withdrawal of forces.
3. Third parties would govern the Islands, temporarily.
4. The two governments would recognise the existence of conflicting viewpoints about the Islands.
5. The two governments would recognise the need to take the viewpoints and interests of the Islanders into account in the final solution.
6. The contact group which would start negotiating at once to implement this agreement would be Brazil, Peru, West Germany and the U.S.
7. A final solution must be found by 30 April 1983 under the contact group's guarantee.

Interim Agreement proposed by HMG (Official Report, 7 May 1982, Vol 23, Col 394

The interim agreement under discussion yesterday included the following elements: first, complete and supervised withdrawal of Argentine forces from the Falkland Islands, matched by corresponding withdrawal of British forces; secondly, an immediate ceasefire as soon as Argentina accepted the agreement and agreed to withdraw; thirdly, appointment of a small group of countries acceptable to both sides which would supervise withdrawal, undertake the interim administration in consultation with the Islanders' elected representatives, and perhaps help in negotiations for a definitive agreement on the status of the islands, without prejudice to our principles or to the wishes of the Islanders; fouthly, suspension of the existing exclusion zones and the lifting of economic sanctions.

Books and Documents referred to in the text

Desmond Rice and Arthur Gavshon, *The Sinking of the Belgrano* (Secker and Warburg 1984)

Brigadier Michael Harbottle O.B.E., *The Peacekeeper's Handbook* (U.N. Training manual.)

"The Falklands Campaign: The Lessons" Cmnd 8758 (HMSO. 1982)

Admiral Sir John Fieldhouse, "Official Despatch of the Task Force Operations Commander", Supplement to *The London Gazette*, 13 December 1982.

Lieutenant Narendra Sethia, "The Sethia Diary"

"Falkland Islands Review" (The Franks Report) Cmnd 8787 (HMSO January 1983.)

Alexander M. Haig, *Caveat: Realism, Reagan and Foreign Policy*, (Weidenfeld 1984)

Hansard: Report of the House of Commons Debate 3 April 1982.

Third Report from the Foreign Affairs Committee (1984-85) "Events Surrounding the Weekend of 1-2 May 1982" (HMSO July 1985)

Hugh Tinker, *Message from the Falklands*, (Junction 1982)

Paul Rogers, "Falkland's Fleet put in Danger" article in *New Statesman*, 3 October 1986

Sara Keays, *Question of Judgement*, (Quintessential 1985)

Steve Berkoff, "Sink the Belgrano!" performed at Halfmoon and Mermaid Theatres September/October 1986

Tam Dalyell, *Thatcher's Torpedo*, (Cecil Woolf 1983)

Tam Dalyell, *Patterns of Deceit*, (Cecil Woolf 1986)

Stockholm International Peace Research Institute, *The Falklands/ Malvinas Conflict*, (Stockholm, SIPRI, 1983)

Duncan Campbell, article on nuclear weapons, *New Statesman* 1984

Duncan Campbell, article on nuclear weapons, *New Statesman* November/ December 1985

Jane's: Fighting Ships, 1982-83 (London 1982)

Government White Paper: "Events Surrounding the Weekend of 1-2 May 1982". Cmnd 9647 (HMSO November 1985)

James Prior *A Balance of Power*, (Hamish Hamilton 1986)

Belgrano Action Group, Enquiry Handbook. (November 1986 — Diana Gould B.A.G.)

Dr. Robert Scheina, "The Malvinas Campaign" reprinted in Appendix 6, The Third F.A.C. Report 1984-85 (HMSO July 1985)

The Minority Report of The Third F.A.C. Report 1984-85 (HMSO July 1985)

Jean Carr, *Another Story, Women and the Falkland's War*, (Hamish Hamilton 1984)

Polly Toynbee, Interviews with Commander O'Connell R.N. *Guardian* articles November 1982 and November 1983

Sunday Times Insight Team, *The Falklands War*, (Sphere 1982)

Ian J. Strange, *The Falklands Islands*, (David and Charles 1983)

John Smith, "74 Days, An Islander's Diary of the Falkland's Occupation" Century 1984)

The Economist, "America's Falklands War," March 1984

Glasgow Media Group, *War and Peace News*, (Open University 1985)

"Relations between Governments, Armed Services and the Media during Times of Armed Conflict" Vol. I (Centre for Journalism Studies, University College, Cardiff, July 1985)

Brian Hanrahan and Robert Fox, *I Counted Them All Out and I Counted Them All Back — The Battle for the Falklands*, (BBC 1982)

John Madeley, "Diego Garcia: a Contrast to the Falklands" (The Minority Rights Group Report, No.54 1982)

Fernando Flores Araoz, in Peruvian Weekly *Oiga*, 27th October 1986.

The Treaty of Tlatelolco is reproduced in *Status of Multilateral Arms Regulation and Disarmament Agreements*, (United Nations).